Driving Demand

Driving Demand

Transforming B2B Marketing to Meet the Needs of the Modern Buyer

Carlos Hidalgo

palgrave
macmillan

DRIVING DEMAND
Copyright © Carlos Hidalgo, 2015.

All rights reserved.

First published in 2015 by
PALGRAVE MACMILLAN®
in the United States—a division of St. Martin's Press LLC,
175 Fifth Avenue, New York, NY 10010.

Where this book is distributed in the UK, Europe and the rest of the world,
this is by Palgrave Macmillan, a division of Macmillan Publishers Limited,
registered in England, company number 785998, of Houndmills,
Basingstoke, Hampshire RG21 6XS.

Palgrave Macmillan is the global academic imprint of the above companies
and has companies and representatives throughout the world.

Palgrave® and Macmillan® are registered trademarks in the United States,
the United Kingdom, Europe and other countries.

ISBN: 978–1–137–52678–6

Library of Congress Cataloging-in-Publication Data

Hidalgo, Carlos (Economist)
    Driving demand : transforming B2B marketing to meet the needs of
    the modern buyer / Carlos Hidalgo.
        pages cm
    Includes index.
    ISBN 978–1–137–52678–6 (alk. paper)
        1. Industrial marketing. 2. Marketing—Technological innovations.
    3. Organizational change. I. Title.

HF5415.1263.H53 2015
658.8′04—dc23   2015015620

A catalogue record of the book is available from the British Library.

Design by Newgen Knowledge Works (P) Ltd., Chennai, India.

First edition: October 2015

10 9 8 7 6 5 4 3 2 1

Contents

Figures

Foreword

"Culture eats strategy for breakfast."

Peter Drucker is often given credit for this insight, which could not be truer when it comes to marketing and B2B organizations. Today, we are seeing vast disruption in a number of business categories, from technology to manufacturing to human resources, but the biggest transformation of all is happening in marketing.

And the pain is visible.

One could argue that the 4 "P's" of place, price, product, and promotion, made popular during the days of Don Draper, are officially dead. Why? Well, there are many reasons, but the biggest is that B2B marketers have no control over the buying process.

Before 1990, there were only eight channels available where a B2B consumer could gather information from a company: an event, a fax, direct mail, telephone, television, radio, billboards, print magazines, and newsletters. Vendors controlled the flow of information, which meant we could predict and staff our teams appropriately to move buyers from awareness to conversion to loyalty.

In 2015, there are literally hundreds of channels where consumers can access content. We've lost control. Some B2B companies have adapted— but most have not.

According to various studies, whether from Forrester or Gartner, anywhere from 60 to 80 percent of the buying process is over before a buyer ever contacts a sales representative. While almost all companies believe this to be true, the basic setup of our sales and marketing organization has not changed. Look at any large B2B company today and you'll find that the sales team still makes demands on marketing, which is considered nothing more than a service group to make more pretty PDF files.

Oh yes, we've added lots of technology, from e-mail to marketing automation to customer relationship management systems. While the belief is that these technologies will help us adapt, the sad truth is that these technologies have become temporary bandages covering up the real issue that always breaks through:

"Culture eats strategy for breakfast."

At Content Marketing Institute, we've had the pleasure of working with more than 100 of the largest B2B companies on the planet. In almost every case, the marketers contacted us not to help them execute a new strategy or understand a new technology but to help them organize and evangelize change. These marketers were frustrated. Their organizations opened up new budgets, threw money at new technology, and kept the exact same processes to sell and market they had used for decades. Their call to us was a cry for help: to stop the insanity.

As you are reading this book, this is your call to arms. For the new process of marketing and demand generation to work in your B2B organization, you need to start doing the little things to aid in transforming your organization based on the truth—the buyers are in control and, for the most part, they don't really care about your products or services. As each day goes by, they will continue to ignore you, regardless of your "amazing" features and benefits.

Right now, smart organizations that understand how to communicate with customers will lead the transformation into a new marketing process. You have the power to make that change. Reading this book is the place to start.

Make change happen. Culture change can happen, and it always starts with one person. That person is you.

Joe Pulizzi
Founder, Content Marketing Institute and
Author, *Epic Content Marketing*

Acknowledgments

Prior to writing this book I spoke to many authors I respect and admire to get their perspectives on authoring a book. I learned a great deal from each of those conversations, but the one common refrain I heard was, "There will be a lot of people to thank when it is all said and done." In the course of writing *Driving Demand*, I have come to realize those people were correct. This book is something I have aspired to do for the past three years, and many have contributed to these ideas and thoughts as well as to my professional development over the years. It is this influence that has enabled me to write what I hope will be a guide for B2B demand generation marketers as we seek to improve our craft. To the following, I give my deepest thanks and gratitude.

First and foremost, I would like to thank my wife, Susanne, who over the past ten years of growing our business has been a tremendous support during the ups and downs of building a company. Your encouragement, love, and support over this time and during this writing process have been most welcomed and so appreciated. I cannot thank you enough!

My kids, Jonathan, Jeremy, Lauren, and Luke: you four are the most amazing kids and have put up with me behind closed doors, pounding away on the keyboard and still think it is cool that dad is writing a book. I so appreciate your patience and encouragement during this process.

My brother Michael: your continual checking in and genuine excitement for me throughout this process along with your words of encouragement and support have been most welcomed and appreciated.

To Adam Needles, my business partner, friend, and sounding board. You are the smartest marketer I have had the pleasure to work with, and many of the thoughts and ideas presented here are ones you have taught me and continue to teach in the work we are doing with our clients.

Jim Woodcock and Jennifer Harmel—thanks for the continual support, words of encouragement, and a listening ear. You two are great partners and ones I am better for knowing and having worked with over these years.

Erika Goldwater, your insights on my writing, your editorial eye, and your ability to translate some of my gibberish into coherent thought in addition to your occasional texts to simply ask "How is it coming?" have made this possible.

To the entire ANNUITAS team: you guys are rock stars, and I would not want to be doing this with anyone else.

To Joe Pulluzi, who wrote the foreword, has been a friend, and a few years ago said, "You have it in your head, now put it down on paper"— thank you.

Thank you also to Ardath Albee, who has been a mentor through the writing process and continually told me "it will be ok."

And also to John Willig, my agent and the one whose patient and steady guidance taught me plenty and brought me here.

To Laurie Harting and the entire Palgrave Macmillan staff for taking a shot at this first-time author and teaching me through this process— thank you.

To the following who have allowed me to pick their brain, offered encouragement, have been friends, sounding boards, and part of my professional and personal development along the way: Michael Burns and Jennifer Green of Michael Burns and Associates, Carla Johnson, Robert Rose, Anne Handley, Brian Kardon, Laura Ramos, Julie Schwartz, Linn Snyder, Nick Panayi, Jon Miller, Craig Rosenberg, Brian Vellmure, Scott Luff, Keith and Michelle Burrows, Larissa DeCarlo, Matt Heinz, Ken Wincko, Steve Gershik, Harold Goldberg, Tracy Thayne, and Warren Cook.

I am sure I have accidentally overlooked some, but I am very thankful to all those who have had a part in this project, and I could not have accomplished this without your support, guidance, and your influence. Thank You!

Introduction

"**M**ost CMOs and marketers I speak to want to change and adapt. But they have a hard time understanding how to change."[1] This statement by *Forbes* columnist David Cooperstein is an all-too-familiar refrain and summarizes much of what is happening in B2B[2] enterprise marketing organizations. I have the opportunity to work and speak with many smart B2B marketing leaders who know they need to change their approach to driving demand in their organizations, but they are at a loss on where to start.

This lack of "understanding how to change" was evidenced in a meeting I had a little more than a year ago when I had lunch with a senior vice president of demand generation for a multibillion dollar software company. This lunch, the first meeting between him and me, was arranged because his company was looking to hire a demand generation agency. "My CEO asked me what was wrong in the company," he stated. "I told him I thought our demand generation was broken, he agreed and told me to fix it, so here we are." So there we were talking about the issues his organization was facing. He began detailing the challenges the company had faced both past and present and how he had previously hired other agencies with little to no success and that this time it had to be different. After about an hour of listening to our approaches to working with our clients, I asked him this question, "While we know there are issues and challenges that you will need to overcome, can we both agree that in order to be successful this endeavor must be about change management and transformation as much as demand generation strategy and the development of content and programs?" With a small grin he said, "You are absolutely right, but how do we move that forward in such a large organization?" This is where they were stuck. The mandate to change was there, the desire to do so was there, but as David Cooperstein stated, making change a reality was missing.

This organization is like many B2B marketing organizations. There is a desire to improve systems, a desire to change, a desire to innovate, but a failure to truly understand what it will take to transform processes that have been in place for years with very little alteration.

Many B2B organizations are investing more, doing more, and creating more content in the name of demand generation; however, it is just more of the same approach and activities with very little result. The Content Marketing Institute[3] reports that 54 percent of companies will either greatly increase or at least increase their spending on content market- ing in the next 12 months. However, even with this increase in spend- ing, only 38 percent state that they are effective with the use of content marketing.

The B2B marketers I encounter are smart, hard-working, driven indi- viduals. However, this practice of simply doing the same thing and spend- ing more money is a common reaction I see throughout B2B enterprise organizations—all with the expectation that this will yield different results. Yet, when the measurement is completed, there is at best incre- mental improvement only.

Many B2B marketers are attempting to transform their demand gener- ation approach and be innovators simply by doing different things; how- ever, they are not really doing things differently—something is lacking.

In order for B2B marketing organizations to fulfill their mandate and drive demand, they need a complete overhaul of their approach to demand generation and their interactions with buyers. First, this over- haul must begin with changing the culture within organizations as there is a desperate need for change management within many B2B market- ing organizations. Second, the approach and mechanisms used to execute demand generation must also change, and the most effective way this will be achieved is by adopting a Demand Process™ approach. This Demand Process Transformation™ requires aligning people, processes, content, and technology to the buyer and the buyer's unique purchase path. This is not a simple fix, but it is a requirement for any marketing organization that wants to drive sustainable revenue, build perpetual programs, and connect with its buyers with relevant, timely dialogue.

This book is intended to be used as a guide for those B2B marketers and leaders who see the need for transforming their demand generation operations and want to adopt a systematic, strategic approach to buyer interaction. This book will not detail "7 Quick and Easy Steps" for marketing leaders to take in order to transform their organization. There are no easy ways to bring about true transformation of this type. This book will not seek to solve all the challenges that face a B2B marketing department; instead, it will focus solely on B2B demand generation. What this book will do is outline the necessary changes that must be made if marketers are to succeed in driving better demand. This book will provide a blueprint for marketing leaders as well as case studies and stories of companies that have adopted this approach, undergone their own transformation, and are now driving sustainable revenues for their businesses.

This book is also a collection of lessons I have learned over the past 20 years of my B2B marketing career as a global director of marketing in the technology world and of working with large enterprise B2B clients over the past ten years as CEO of ANNUITAS.

I have not mentioned by name all of the companies in some of the examples and at times will change names, as I am not using these stories as a means of "calling out" an organization or an individual; rather, these learning examples are provided in the hope that other B2B marketing professionals can relate and apply these learnings to their situation.

My hope is that through this book, B2B demand generation professionals and marketing leaders will see that this change is no longer optional; it is a requirement that our businesses and our sophisticated buyers demand. I trust that this book serves not only as a prescriptive road map for those driving change in their organizations but also as motivation for others to begin leading their organizations down the road to transformation.

Having worked in B2B marketing for over two decades, I believe there is no better time to be a B2B marketer than now. Our organizations from the CEO on down are demanding more from us and relying more on us, and never before has there been a better opportunity for those in the B2B marketing profession to impact our organizations and for marketing leaders to gain that ever elusive "seat at the table." The only missing ingredient in most organizations is change.

CHAPTER 1

The Issues with Modern Demand Generation

Several years ago, Eloqua (now Oracle) ushered in the phrase *Modern Marketing*. The term was meant to indicate that B2B marketing is in a new era, that we have the tools and the means to market in this Internet-enabled and social age we live in. While we are certainly in the midst of a modern era, few organizations are making the necessary adjustments to equip their people to be "Modern Marketers" and are not keeping pace with what is needed in demand generation today. As buyers now have access to more information via the Internet and social media, their approach to buying is growing more sophisticated and complex. Rather than looking for information from the vendor's sales reps, they are finding this information on their own and taking more control of their buying journey. As a result, vendors and sales people often do not become involved until much later in the buying cycle.

In the 2014 Enterprise B2B Demand Generation study[1] launched by my firm ANNUITAS, only 2.8 percent of respondents rated themselves as highly effective when it came to "achieving their Demand Generation goals and objectives." Additionally, the CEB reported that leads that are created from B2B demand generation programs "only convert zero to three percent of the time."[2] That is, while our buyers are becoming more modern in their approach, the majority of marketers are failing to keep pace in terms of sophistication.

In my experience and based on what I hear daily from B2B marketers, there are some consistent and common challenges that are causing this stagnation, and there is a struggle to advance beyond isolated tactics and marginally effective campaigns. B2B marketers are far behind their buyers in terms of sophistication and in order to catch up they need to fundamentally change their model and approach to overcome the common problems that negatively impact most organizations.

A Strategic versus Tactical Approach to Demand Generation

I recently had a discussion with the chief marketing officer (CMO) of a new client, a large publically traded technology company. The CMO explained to me that her team had met its lead goals for the first half of the year, but in the most recent board meeting she was "beaten up" by the chief executive officer (CEO) and head of sales because marketing had not provided the expected value. Her only defense was "we exceeded the number of leads at the top of the funnel and that is the metric by which my team is measured." However, after our team had conducted some analysis of our client's campaigns, it was revealed that the sales close rate on leads generated by marketing was an anemic .8 percent. Obviously, there was a disconnect between what her team was doing on a day-to-day basis and what the organization expected and needed.

This scenario is not foreign to many B2B marketers I speak to. They are driving a lot of "top of funnel" engagement and are passing on those leads to sales, but they are doing very little beyond that to enable the sales team to close leads at a higher conversion rate. This issue is perpetuated because organizations continue to take a very campaign-driven or tactical approach to generating demand. In the 2014 B2B Enterprise Demand Generation study conducted by ANNUITAS, over 60 percent of respondents stated that they run more than 15 campaigns on an annual basis, and studies by Forrester and Content Marketing Institute show similar numbers. These campaigns typically center on an asset or an event. In a typical scenario, an asset is created, such as a white paper, eBook, video, etc., and then the marketing team posts these assets on the corporate website, sends e-mails to a targeted list promoting the asset, and perhaps even shares it on social media. Those potential buyers who download the asset are then considered leads, and their contact information sent to the sales team, Those who did not respond are sent another round of e-mails (this process is often mistakenly referred to as *nurturing*) a report is generated to show the number of "leads" generated, and then it's off to the next campaign—promoting a booth at a trade show, pushing new content, or preparing for an upcoming webinar. And so the cycle continues, leading to missed opportunities to connect with buyers and producing very little in the way of return on investment (ROI). This tactical, campaign-driven approach only serves to create a gap in the middle (nurture stage) of the funnel (see figure 1.1), which is the critical stage in any program. This is where most leads are lost and where chances of a successful program begin to unravel.

Rather than take this tactical approach, B2B marketers need to take a strategic approach to demand generation. Strategic demand generation is defined as follows: "A perpetual process that is both operationalized and optimized to Engage, Nurture, and Convert both prospects and customers along their buying process. A process that is designed to educate and qualify through the collaboration of marketing and sales activities with the goal of driving revenue and maximizing customer lifetime *value*."[3] This is a radical departure from the typical one-and-done tactical campaign approach that many organizations practice. However, taking a

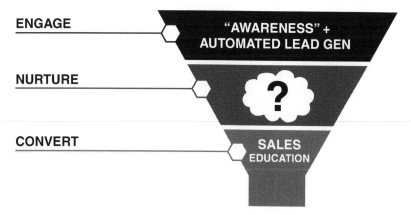

Figure 1.1 Mid-Funnel Gap Caused by a Campaign-Driven Approach.

strategic, buyer-centric approach to demand generation will drastically improve results and have a positive impact on corporate revenue.

Organizations Lead with Technology

Gartner's 2012 prediction that by the year 2017 CMOs[4] would spend more money on technology than chief information officers (CIOs) served to stir B2B marketers and marketing technology vendors into a frenzy. At last count, according to Scott Brinker at ChiefMartec, there were over 1,876 marketing technology vendors,[5] and this list is expected to grow over the next several years. However, even with all of this technology and budget to spend, very few marketers are able to demonstrate real value deriving from their investments.

In the ANNUITAS B2B Enterprise Demand Generation study, less than 21 percent of those who own marketing automation claimed to have been successful at achieving their goals with this technology. And this aligns with what I hear from most of the customers and clients I have the opportunity to work with. Companies have owned marketing automation, social media tools, and other technologies for a number of years, and yet they are still not much further along in demonstrating the return on their marketing investment than they were before. Recently, I spoke to one director of demand generation at a billion-dollar health care company, and he said, "We have two Ferraris parked in our parking lot, Marketo for marketing automation and Salesforce.com for CRM, yet we need someone to come in and teach us how to drive them." His company is like so many others who have made technology the focal point of their demand generation plans rather than seeing it as an enabler of the strategy that needs to be developed first. When marketing technology becomes the starting point of any program, that program is doomed to fail because technology alone cannot drive strategy or deliver perpetual demand.

Organizations Are Not Truly Connecting with Their Buyers

In their 2013 B2B Content Preferences Survey, DemandGen Report asked B2B buyers to rate how well vendors were doing with their content. In the survey, 62 percent of buyers strongly agreed that vendors focus their content too much on product specifications and not enough on value. The same study asked buyers to rank vendors on "organizing and presenting relevant content on their websites," and less than half the respondents stated that vendors are doing a good job; only 5 percent rated vendors as doing an excellent job.[6] Clearly, there is still work to be done.

The approach that many organizations take to get closer to their buyers is a rather insular one where workshops abound. Well-meaning marketers plan sessions, at times with the help of an outside consultant, and get marketing and sales teams together to create buyer personas and map out the buyers' journey. The problem with this approach is that it is only as good as the insights from the room, which offer only the one-sided view of the vendors' perception of their buyer. These sessions provide a useful view into the steps buyers take on the macro level, but workshops do not provide the necessary detail to align content to each and every stage of the buying process.

Before working with my team, one of my clients had spent approximately 10 percent of the company's marketing budget with an agency to develop a social media strategy. The CMO and vice president of marketing were convinced they needed this to connect with their buyers and to thus improve their demand generation. As part of our process to collect buyer insights for the creation of a strategic demand generation program, we started with interviewing the company's buyers and others who were not their customers but had the same buyer profile. In the interviews we asked, "What channels do you and your colleagues use when gathering content and data to make an informed purchase decision?" We heard many different answers: Google, the vendor website, response to e-mails, webinars, etc. However, the one thing that was never mentioned by any of the interviewees was social media. When we asked, "Do you use social media?" The answer was a resounding no. It is important to note that the client we were working with sold its products to service centers and customer support organizations. As one of the interviewees told me, "The new way to complain about lousy service is social media; it is the bane of my existence, and other than responding to it for my job, I do not and will not use it in any way shape or form." Other answers in the interviews were not all that declarative but expressed the same thought. That is, our client's buyers were not using this channel; yet our client had failed to take an outside, buyer-centric view. As a result, a large amount of money was being wasted on the social media strategy the company's marketing team felt it had to have.

Interviewing buyers is paramount to uncovering the entire buying process, which includes buyers' content consumption patterns (where and how they consume content and their content preferences), having a deep understanding of who in the buyers' organization is involved in the purchase process, identifying the "trigger event" that moves buyers into a purchase process and understanding the problems they are looking to solve. Businesses wanting to understand the audience they are selling to also need to interview those who fit their ideal prospect profile, but are not necessarily their customers as they will provide additional information that is not biased toward the sellers brand. The key to these interviews is to develop questions that are not focused on why buyers bought a product from you as a vendor, but that lead you to insights into the buyers' intent without any bias toward your organization. Asking questions such as, "What were the first steps you took when you began the buying process? Who in the organization kicked off the buying process? What were the next steps after the buying process began? What were the events that started the purchase process?" These kinds of open-ended questions will provide insight over and above what marketing, sales teams and a customer database can provide.

The missing piece in being able to develop the insights into buyers is research. This is one area that more often than not most B2B marketers ignore. Understanding the market conditions in which your buyer lives on a day-to-day basis will help craft the messaging that will educate and inform buyers along their purchasing journey. Think about the impact Obamacare had on the health care market. How did this new legislation impact those in the health care market and how purchase decisions are made in this vertical? Did this new legislation create a new buying trigger for certain health care and insurance buyers? I spoke with one health care provider who told me that since the passage of the Affordable Care Act buyers are involving more people in the purchase of their products, and the sales cycles have grown longer.

Once all of these steps are taken (interviews, research, etc.), then that marketers can begin to create relevant and personal content that is aligned with how the buyers buy as opposed to how the seller wants to sell. While this approach requires more effort and work than a typical asset-focused, tactical campaign, the shift in B2B buyers' purchase patterns calls for this new approach; the old, traditional approach just isn't working anymore.

A Siloed Organizational Approach

The organizational structure of most B2B marketing departments is a detriment to building strategic, perpetual demand generation programs that drive revenue. In my work with enterprise organizations, I find nearly all of them are organized into silos. Departments are defined based on activity or channels, for example, a marketing automation team, events team, social media team, web team, etc. The prevailing problem with this kind of organizational makeup is that no department addresses the buyers' entire purchase path, and as a result content continuity for buyers' engagement with the vendor is lacking. I was discussing this problem with a vice president of marketing at an enterprise telecommunications company whose team was responsible for lead nurturing. As she put it, "My team is responsible for developing campaigns for the middle of the funnel." She agreed that this was a very difficult assignment as there was another team responsible for "top of funnel" engagement and yet another team responsible for sales enablement once the lead was passed along to sales. The struggle was clarifying what content was used and producing metrics to prove the value of her team's lead nurturing activity. "It is very hard for us to collaborate due to the fact we are all so busy just trying to execute on our areas of responsibility," she stated. "We develop tactics that we think will work. In reality, the whole process is broken, and it is nearly impossible to derive any meaningful measurements from our work." She understood that even her team's best efforts at developing content would not work if her department, along with others, was not fully aligned with buyers and their purchase stages.

Robert Rose, chief strategy officer for the Content Marketing Institute, explained in an interview that businesses react to the digital disruption with siloed approaches.[7] "The number of teams that exist to address this single stratum is overwhelming. We have stratified the sales funnel to such an extent that we have created efforts that only address and measure that stratification. The demand generation team is a great example—they have their own budget, their own platform, their own agency, and while they are working on their plans, they do not communicate with brand, social, etc. These teams manage just their own world and exist in their own silos. This situation is untenable and not scalable." This approach of "organizational stratification" is certainly not scalable, and it limits the ability of B2B marketers to effectively create demand and drive pipeline and revenue. Rather than simply reacting to the B2B digital disruption, organizations need a planned approach that allows for a distributed span of control over demand generation. This approach breaks down the silos and calls for organizing demand around the various buyer groups that may be relevant buyer targets for a business. As Rose commented, "The good companies that I have seen *(early adopters)* are beginning to align the various stratifications, reduce the number of agencies, align groups, align activities, and integrate across the various marketing disciplines in order to have a better connection point to their buyers."

Lack of Skill Set

In their July 2013 report *B2B CMOs Must Evolve of Move On,*[8] Forrester took a look at the ever evolving role of the CMO. The report stated the following:

- 96 percent of CMOs either agreed or strongly agreed that "the breadth of skills needed to succeed in marketing has increased dramatically"
- 56 percent of CMOs either agreed or strongly agreed that "it is increasingly difficult to train staff adequately on the skills needed to market our business"

This lack of skill set is one more issue that B2B marketing leaders must face. As the digital disruption continues, the skills that are needed are in very short supply. In the ANNUITAS study, when participants were asked to "rate the skill set of their marketing personnel in terms of executing demand generation strategy," only 7.5 percent of respondents rated their teams as "highly skilled." This lack of the needed skills is only highlighted in that very few universities are educating their marketing graduates in the newest skills required in the new world of B2B demand generation. Last year, when I spoke at a university about the new age of marketing, a junior marketing major asked me what the term B2B meant. His school, like many, is still not teaching B2B marketing, which is contributing to the widening skills gap.

Organizations need to make the necessary investments to equip their marketing personnel with the new skills and knowledge that enables marketers to practice their craft effectively. As part of this process, B2B marketing departments should look into either getting this training through an organization and thus educate their personnel individually or developing their own professional development organization. This type of enablement has been commonplace for sales teams in most B2B organizations for years, and the same should be created for marketing teams. Marketing enablement is important for teams to become successful, especially now that marketing has taken on strategic significance.

Not Involving Sales

Demand generation is not just a marketing activity. While the role of sales in B2B purchases has been altered significantly due to the change in buying patterns, the inclusion of sales in the development and execution of demand generation is severely lacking in most organizations. According to the ANNUITAS study, the majority of B2B demand generation professionals are not working with sales teams to enhance their demand generation results:

- Only 41.5 percent of B2B demand generation teams routinely involve sales staff in the development of their buyer personas.
- Only 21.7 percent of B2B demand generation teams have a "collaborative, involved" approach with sales teams in the development of their demand generation strategies.

- Only 29.3 percent of B2B organizations have a common set of key performance indicators (KPIs) that both marketing and sales share to measure success

By not working with the sales teams, marketers run the risk of putting in plenty of effort with very little return from within the organization. In one of the first client companies I worked with at ANNUITAS, this issue profoundly affected the company's demand generation results. The corporation's director of marketing walked me through the marketing programs and strategy for the coming year. He also showed me the lead definitions and service level agreements (SLAs) his team had developed and informed me that "all of this had been agreed to by sales." After that, I met with the vice president of sales and some of his directors to hear their insights into the status of demand generation at the company. During this meeting I mentioned the demand generation strategy, the lead definitions, and SLAs that had been defined. They had no idea what I was referring to. I explained what I had just seen and that I had been informed that there was agreement between marketing and sales departments. One of the sales directors chuckled and explained that the sales teams never saw what was coming from marketing until after the campaigns had been launched and that most of the time they just ignored the leads generated from the marketing campaigns. From his perspective, marketing did not have the insights into the buyers to develop the right campaigns. Furthermore, most of marketing's "leads" were not really qualified to the level needed so this sales director felt responding to anything was a waste of time; therefore, he had instructed his teams to focus on generating their own quality leads and not worry about marketing. His tone was not combative in any way, but he knew his job was to sell, and he was going to put his energy into what helped him accomplish the goal at hand. If marketing was not going to work together with the sales department to help accomplish that goal, then he and his colleagues would just work on their own.

This lack of alignment is not that uncommon in B2B enterprise organizations. Marketing departments get so focused on developing content, executing campaigns, and dealing with day-to-day tasks that they fail to engage the sales departments in the development of strategy and content. While demand generation should be spearheaded by marketing, not having an active collaboration with sales teams and not including their unique insights into the market and buyers will limit the effectiveness of demand generation and also limit the uptake of sales.

A Lack of Complete Ownership

A few years ago I met with a new client who wanted us to develop and implement a buyer-centric demand generation strategy. In our first meeting with the vice president and some members of her team, we reviewed their personas and some of the new content that had been developed. It became clear very quickly that much of the content and the personas that had been created were not useful for demand generation. The personas focused more on the demographic of an individual and not on buying triggers, challenges, or roles in the buying decision. The content was also lacking in its educational focus (as opposed to focus on product) and would not be useful in helping a buyer make a more informed decision. As we continued the meeting it was revealed that corporate marketing was responsible for developing the content and the personas. I asked why the demand generation team did not have a greater role in this and was told that the company wanted the content function centralized and that corporate marketing was a shared service across the organization. Our client agreed that the demand generation team was not getting what it needed, but the decision had come from the CMO. There was no chance to change it even though the demand generation specificity was not there.

Many companies are struggling with demand generation today even when they have a demand generation team in place because so often that team is still not given the tools or control needed to carry out its tasks with precision. The responsibility for this situation lies with other groups, most often with the corporate marketing department.

In looking at how companies approach demand generation, the ANNUITAS study found the following:

- 39.6 percent of companies state that the corporate marketing department is responsible for the development of buyer personas, and only 29.3 percent say this is the responsibility of the demand generation team.
- 61.3 percent of companies state that the corporate marketing department is responsible for the creation of content, and only 31.1 percent state that this is the responsibility of the demand generation team.[9]

Demand generation in the age of sophisticated, contemporary buyers requires specific skills, specific characteristics within personas, and specific content for each stage of the buyers' journey, and yet overwhelmingly organizations are delegating the task of demand generation to other departments within marketing. Then they expect the demand generation teams to assemble everything and show results. Currently, only 37.7 percent of B2B enterprise organizations have a team specifically dedicated to all aspects of demand generation.[10]

Not long ago, I was invited by a company (now a client) to a global marketing meeting of vice presidents and marketing executives. During the day-long event the executives discussed what they called their "marketing supply chain." In this supply chain model, various groups had certain roles, and once they had done their part, they would exit the process with the expectation that the next team would perform its task until there was a finished product that could be executed as a campaign. After the presentation, the senior vice president of demand generation asked me "What do you think?" I responded by asking, "Who owns it?" In this supply chain model it was not clear who owned or who was responsible for end-to-end demand generation, and the results were indicative of that.

For demand generation to be successful, there needs to be an owner. Organizations cannot add this function to other departments simply because corporate marketers most likely do not know what needs to be done to activate perpetual, buyer-centric demand generation. Developing a team dedicated to this discipline, however, will provide the results organizations expect from their investments in demand generation.

Advancing Demand Generation to a Modern State

If B2B marketers are going to achieve a more modern approach, these common challenges must be addressed. Operationalizing and optimizing people, processes, content, and technology to focus on buyers and their purchase path is the only way organizations will overcome the tactical rut they are currently in. Adopting a demand process approach should become a top priority for marketing leaders who want to get more from their marketing and sales investments and have a greater impact on their business.

CHAPTER 2

Leading Demand Process Transformation

I met with representatives of an international manufacturing company who wanted to change their approach to demand generation. They had one of the leading marketing automation and CRM tools, had invested significantly in marketing campaigns and the development of content, and had worked with three different agencies over the previous three years. In their words, they "had very little to show for it." Our meeting was the result of their team attending a speech I gave on the need for a change in B2B marketing. As we began our meeting, the director said, "We do not need just another agency, we have tried that already. We truly need to do things differently and change the approach if we are going to be effective." This organization knew its marketing was not effective and that simply bringing in a new agency and creating more content or pushing out additional campaigns was not enough; the executives understood that change was imperative, but they were stuck.

Demand Process Transformation

For marketing leaders looking to make changes in their approach to demand generation that yield results, they need to adopt a Demand Process approach to their demand generation. Demand Process is the practice of aligning people (marketing and sales), processes, content, and technology to that of buyers and their buying process. It is a holistic approach that ensures demand generation starts with the buyer and is the core of all demand generation programs. At a more granular level, Demand Process includes the following attributes:

- *Buyer-Centric:* Aligning **all** marketing and sales interactions to B2B buyers and their buying process. This includes developing demand generation content, programs, and systems that align to the buyers' buying process. Being buyer-centric means eliminating one-off campaigns that revolve around a specific asset (white paper, e-book) or event (trade show or webinar).
- *Revenue-Oriented:* This focuses all demand generation activity on delivering revenue and maximizing customer lifetime value (CLV) rather than driving volume for potential leads. This requires taking a strategic and outcome-oriented approach to identifying, qualifying, and converting B2B buyers in a repeatable, predictable, and programmatic fashion. The focus on revenue is often discussed, but something that many CMOs still grapple with or shy away from altogether. One CMO told me, "I do not want to begin committing to driving pipeline and revenue, that's a scary proposition." However, this is necessary for true transformation.
- *Integrated and Orchestrated:* All demand generation activities must be operationalized. This includes developing a sequence of Engagement, Nurturing, and Conversion of the buyer, a series of steps that is closely managed and optimized and thus leads to revenue.

This approach is the only way organizations will build sustainable, perpetual, and revenue-generating demand generation programs.

Today's B2B buyers are more sophisticated and have access to more information than ever before; they are no longer dependent on vendors to educate and inform them about their products and solutions. In today's digital age buyers take a different approach (57 percent of the buying process is complete before the buyer engages with the vendor[1]), it is necessary to ensure that there is a next step beyond the initial engagement. The goal of any organization should be to establish an ongoing dialogue with buyers and customers that aligns to their needs and challenges along the

Figure 2.1   Engage, Nurture, Convert Approach to Demand Generation.

path buyers take to purchase. This cannot be done simply by engaging buyers at the top of the sales funnel. It is absolutely necessary that B2B demand generation professionals seek to Engage, Nurture, and Convert (see figure 2.1) their buyers. As seen in the previous chapter, when organizations fail to take a holistic approach to interacting with their buyers and customers, a gap opens in the middle of the funnel, nurturing becomes an entirely separate activity there. As a result, there is no continuity of dialogue. Consequently, the conversation between buyer and vendor is then broken off, and this leads to a poor buying experience.

When organizations adopt a Demand Process approach, nurturing is viewed as a strategic phase of the ongoing conversation. Nurturing becomes the bridge between top-of-funnel engagement and the eventual interaction with the sales team (convert stage).

Along the continuum of Engage, Nurture, and Convert, there will be many touchpoints as the B2B buying process is very rarely a linear, funnel-like process. In most buying processes, there will be many interactions or information requests (IR) from buyers as they continue toward their purchase decision. In response to this, it is imperative that B2B organizations think about how this impacts their content and the various channels used and how they need to align to what the buyers need at each stage.

Content in the Engage stage must focus on the buyers' top-of-mind issues. At this stage on their path to purchase, buyers are looking for answers to their questions and challenges. Organizations should develop content that speaks to top-of-mind issues and challenges in an educational way without pushing their brand or product on buyers.

Content in the Nurturing stage is designed to move from the buyers' top-of-mind challenges to solution categories; this content points out the different areas where the vendor can assist buyers in meeting their challenges. Throughout the Nurture stage, buyers should be progressively profiled and scored so there is an indication as to when they are ready to speak to a sales representative.

Content for the Convert stage is driven in large part by the sales team; however, it is produced by the marketing team and at certain times can be automated via the integration of marketing automation and CRM. However, conversion content takes into account the buyers' previous interactions and is a continuation of the dialogue that buyers had in the Engage and Nurture stages. For all these stages multiple channels can be used, and marketers should determine what channels are most effective and preferred by buyers.

The alignment of content to the continuum of Engage, Nurture, and Convert is fundamental to Demand Process. However, organizations cannot stop at simply retooling their approach to content as that will bring only minimal gains. For organizations to realize the benefits of true transformation, they need to fully operationalize the demand generation function and align the people, processes, and technology (see figure 2.2) with the content.

By operationalizing these four key areas, organizations ensure that buyers are the focus of all that occurs in the demand generation function and also make sure they have a cohesive strategy. Each of the areas in the architecture serves to support and enable the others, and this provides

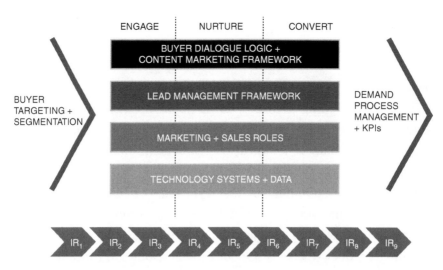

Figure 2.2 ANNUITAS Demand Process Architecture.

a seamless buying experience for buyers and much higher quality leads for the sales team. All too often, organizations look at each of the pillars of this architecture separately, and as a result, they fail to see any true change or increase in overall value. Only when the issue is approached holistically can organizations see sustainable revenues that maximize CLV and ROI.

Taking a Pilot Approach

The number one question people ask me when I speak to a large B2B enterprise organization about moving to a Demand Process approach is where to start. These large organizations do not have the luxury of stopping the "marketing machine," but they see the need for changing their approach. They must carry out the change while also keeping their demand generation engine running. Adding to the challenge, the majority of enterprise organizations are very complex organizations comprising multiple product lines, solution areas, and lines of business; they support multiple geographies and have many audience segments that align to specific product lines and solutions. How does such an organization adopt a Demand Process approach and ensure that it becomes predominant across a global organization?

The most effective way an organization can begin this process of leading Demand Process Transformation™ is to pilot this approach. By selecting a line of business, audience segment, or solution area, organizations can test this new approach without slowing down any of the other activities in the rest of the business. There are several advantages to taking this pilot approach to Demand Process:

- It allows the business to continue operating as before while the one selected area is "trying on" the new approach and adapting to a new model. This approach is minimally disruptive to the organization but enables this one selected area to learn and spread the insights gained to the whole of the business.
- The pilot approach functions as the prototype for change. As the pilot begins to take shape, the fundamental elements that are established

serve as the blueprint the organization to follow as it seeks to change its entire approach to demand generation.

- Those who are involved in the pilot are educated and are able to improve their demand generation skill and expertise. These individuals then serve as champions of change when organizations begin to roll out the new demand process across the entire enterprise.

In selecting the optimal business area for a pilot initiative, it is best to consider those segments that offer opportunities for improvement and a high potential for a win—that is, areas showing lagging sales, low market penetration, poor quality or volume of leads, and so on. Moreover, it is imperative that both marketing and sales departments are committed to the initiative because demand generation is a function of both groups. If the sales teams are not on board with this new approach and insist on continuing with the status quo, then it's best to find another business area for running the pilot program since this resistance will lead to failure.

Within the framework of the pilot program, organizations must ensure that all the components of the Demand Process are implemented and can be operated in a different function from the rest of the business. This most likely means that within this pilot initiative, lead qualification, lead scoring, service level agreements, and the handoff of leads from marketing to the sales group must be different from what is common practice in the rest of the organization. This difference will also impact the use of technology and the configuration of marketing and sales systems. Without making changes to their full extent within the pilot, organizations cannot properly assess the value of this new approach.

Organizations that have undergone Demand Process Transformation are benefitting from strategic, perpetual programs that are driving pipeline contribution and revenue. These marketing organizations are able to report on ROI and show the business the impact they are making through the investment of marketing dollars. What follows is a case study of an organization my team has worked with as it adopted this buyer-centric, modern demand generation approach; the company has benefitted from the positive impact of this change.

PR Newswire Case Study

PR Newswire is the premier global provider of multimedia platforms that enable marketers, corporate communicators, sustainability officers, public affairs officers, and investor relations officers to leverage content to engage with their key audiences. Having pioneered the commercial news distribution industry 58 years ago, PR Newswire today provides end-to-end solutions to produce, optimize, and target content—from rich media to online video to multimedia—and then distribute content and measure results across traditional, digital, mobile and social channels. PR Newswire serves tens of thousands of clients from offices in the Americas, Europe, Middle East, Africa, and the Asia-Pacific region, and is a UBM plc company.

Before Demand Process

Prior to adopting a Demand Process approach, demand generation could be described in the following ways according to Ken Wincko, senior vice president of marketing for PR Newswire:

- A demand generation strategy was a campaign approach that included a start and stop. It was an intermittent, one-off approach. As Wincko put it, "We would run a campaign that may have a certain theme, but there was nothing perpetual. Once the campaign was completed, we would develop another one."
- There was a focus on only two or three channels. Organizations relied heavily on e-mail marketing and a few events and invested in pay-per-click (PPC) advertising as well, but none of these activities were integrated, and there was no unified multichannel approach.
- The campaign approach was not buyer-centric. There was no time or research spent on defining the audience segments, understanding the needs of the buyers or their journey to purchase.

This approach failed to produce meaningful results, and marketing and sales departments became more disconnected. According to Wincko, "There was certainly the old theme of sales wanting higher quality and marketing saying they are delivering. This continued to drive a divide between the two departments." The relationship between marketing and sales departments suffered in part because no lead prioritization had been established. Leads that were passed on had no context or value tied to them because most of these leads were just names. "It was as if sales was calling into a cold list of names when they would respond to a lead," stated Wincko. "This put our sales team into a very transactional mode of selling as they were calling at random into a name, but we [marketing] were calling them leads. Sales had every right to be concerned with the quality of the leads, as marketing was not delivering a lot of value and did not know how to get there. They did not understand the shift that was going on in the marketplace and the need to get there."

The Decision to Transform

There were several key decisions to be made to initiate transformation in the organization. The CEO of the organization recognized that the PR (public relations) industry is undergoing significant transformation. These changes together with significant competitive pressures had caused the slowing of overall revenues. Together, the CEO, Wincko and his team realized that marketing could serve as a catalyst for the organization and enable the business to respond in a way that would allow it to take advantage of some untapped opportunities. They also believed that marketing was not taking advantage of the organization's new technologies and had not fully adapted to a digital approach.

The organization had used one of the leading marketing automation solutions for the previous three years, but it was still not clear on how best to utilize the solution and integrate it with other channels. Wincko and the members of his team also knew they needed to look beyond marketing automation and review the structure of the marketing organization, its approach to data governance, and its engagement with buyers.

In addition, in order to ensure this transformation would be successful, new leadership was needed. Historically, marketing and sales departments reported to one leader and in order to oversee the remodeling that was needed, PR Newswire made the decision to separate these responsibilities and bring in Wincko as the new leader to oversee the marketing change that was needed. Having one only person in charge of managing sales and driving global revenue while also managing and driving a wholesale change in marketing was not feasible.

Once Wincko was appointed to lead the marketing organization, he worked with the leader of the sales teams to forge a partnership and collaborate toward tighter alignment between the two departments. The two groups needed to move from working in silos in a transactional manner to becoming more strategic so they could achieve better results.

The Path to Transformation

With the decision to change made at the highest levels of the organization, the process began quickly. The first step was building a plan for the first 90 days of the endeavor, and Wincko looked to address four key areas to ensure at the outset that the initiative had clear goals and objectives

Technology: PR Newswire's marketers saw that they were not getting the most from their marketing and sales technologies. Specifically, they analyzed their use of marketing automation and how it was utilized; they found it was mainly used as an e-mail engine. However, as their buyers were engaging in multiple channels, they needed to expand the use of their automation beyond e-mail and move to a multichannel demand generation approach.

Data: Wincko and his team understood the value of good data and knew that if they had inaccurate data, their demand generation programs would suffer. "We recognized that the data was crucial, it needed to be clean, and at the time we started this process, it was pretty poor as data integrity was not something the organization had focused on before," said Wincko. In order to address this issue, PR Newswire created an alignment between the CIO and the marketing department that led to the creation of a task force to address this issue. The result was the implementation of a data hygiene policy and the development of governance standards for the management of marketing data.

Content: With the understanding that PR Newswire was going to move away from its traditional one-off campaign approach, the marketers needed to define their content strategy. As Wincko put it, "This move from one-off to perpetual demand caused us to really define the philosophy we would take to demand generation." Rather than just create more content, PR Newswire has now moved to a Demand Process model where research and interviews with customers and prospective buyers are conducted to understand the various buyer segments, define the buyer personas, and enable the marketing team to get a close look at the buyers' journey by segment and persona. The next step is to create a content architecture that aligns to the buyers' journey for each segment and buyer persona. As Wincko notes, "This was a critical piece for us in terms of defining the overall strategy."

People: Wincko and his team also looked that the way the marketing team was structured. They examined the roles and responsibilities in the organization to see whether they were aligned to their buyers' approach to purchasing. Thinking like this led the marketers to restructure the demand generation team. Rather than organizing the team by functional roles, they aligned the roles to those of their buyer segments to better support the new process.

Process: In order to continually optimize this approach and their demand generation programs, Wincko and his colleagues wanted to ensure the organization would be agile: "We knew we would be building more of these programs for multiple segments and personas, which would necessitate more content. We needed to be sure to do this in an agile way as the reporting, optimization, and analysis of these programs would guide our investments going forward."

Overcoming Potential Roadblocks to Change

One of the first things Wincko and his colleagues recognized in the organization was the amount of waste occurring. Many in the marketing department were focusing on their own tasks and goals, but there was no accountability in terms of measurement or success. Moving the team to think in a framework was the first hurdle to overcome. "We needed to make behavioral changes within the organization," stated Wincko. "We were changing the model to move from a siloed approach to that of a collaborative team. In addition, the people who previously had no measurement applied to their work were now going to be held accountable for their efforts, and this caused some hesitation and resistance. In order to move to a performance-based organization, behavior had to be modified.

The challenge, however, was not just to get people in the marketing department to change, but there was work to be done across the organization at the leadership level as well. Wincko needed to shape the behavior of his peers (CEO, CFO) and get them to believe in the vision of where marketing and demand generation were headed to get the necessary investments of money and people to move forward. Moreover, Wincko had to get people in other departments to see that this transformation could be accomplished while mitigating the risks to the business. The need to align and have a common vision with the other department heads and not have this initiative driven solely by the marketing department was crucial to the overall success of the pilot and the future vision of transformation.

Part of this transformational process was developing a business case for the investment, which is ongoing. However, since launching its first demand generation pilot program, PR Newswire has seen results showing that the Demand Process approach works and can be a revenue driver for the organization: over 240 new deals were closed as a result of the strategic program including an incremental lift of an 8 percent increase in qualified leads and 5 percent increase in closed deals. Another outcome of the changes is that the perception of marketing has changed internally; before marketing had been seen as a cost center, and now it is viewed as a profit center for the business.

The talent and skills in the organization were also a crucial component of PR Newswire's success. As Wincko explains, "We needed to bring in the people who understood perpetual demand generation and what we are trying to accomplish as a team. Even if they had never really done it before, we brought in people who understand the changing dynamics in the market and who would be able to pick up the buyer-centric approach quickly."

Wincko also knew that an external change agent was critical to ensuring this process became part of the marketing department's DNA. As Wincko puts it, "Having a third party to help us through this process has enabled us to move much faster than if we had tried to do this by ourselves. An outside partner is critical to gaining internal support and has helped us drive this change in a matter of months rather than years if we had gone it alone."

Building a Culture of Change

Once the potential roadblocks were identified, Wincko began to evangelize the vision of becoming a performance-based, accountable, innovative, buyer-aligned organization. This vision was brought to every level in the marketing organization, and as quick wins occurred, Wincko and his team evangelized them as a way to get others to also buy into the vision. He brought in new talent with the requisite skills to effectively manage each stage of the demand generation process aligned to the buyer's journey. In addition, he has focused on providing ample training and educational opportunities for his team which has increased the overall skill level.

The Impact of Transformation

The results that have been realized from this transformation have been significant. First and foremost, PR Newswire's relationship with its buyers has improved significantly. The feedback from sales teams shows that their job is easier when responding to leads because they are now engaged with buyers in a way that they never were before. In addition, the conversion rates along the buying funnel have improved significantly. The conversion rate from contact at the engaged stage to qualified opportunities is 17.65 percent, which is almost three times of what is best-in-class standard.

Marketing and sales teams are also now working in a collaborative fashion. Wincko highlights, "We [marketing] are taking the buyers halfway through the buyers' journey and providing sales buyer insights into this process. There are no more cold calls from sales. When sales engages with a marketing-generated prospect, they know the path the buyer took, their pain points, challenges, and objectives. The conversations with prospects now have a lot more context, and sales are seeing more value from marketing." Since embarking on the path to transformation, the members of the sales force have been closing over 50 percent of the qualified leads they are receiving from the strategic demand generation programs, and marketing is now taking this strategic demand generation approach to other business segments in the organization.

Shared Advice

Wincko hopes that other B2B organizations will follow PR Newswire's approach and begin their own organizational transformation. He advises that any change initiative will be complex and must be looked at holistically and through a variety of lenses. What will help achieve results is getting an outside organization to guide and direct this significant initiative. Overall, from Wincko's perspective, the change is about being fearless. "It is about having a strong vision and taking the leap of faith. You have to keep iterating based on the analytics and keep working to improve every day. It won't be an easy process. Get your teams and your peers on board and drive change—otherwise you risk getting left behind."

CHAPTER 3

Why Transformation Fails

In 2014, B2B marketers were asked to rate the most important "soft skills" needed for the "Skills of the Modern Marketer,"[1] and the number one response was "the ability to embrace change" with 75 percent of the respondents ranking this as the highest priority. With the majority of organizations ranking this skill as the top one, why are so many organizations struggling with the ability to transform? I've met with many marketers and marketing leaders who understand that what has worked in the past is no longer effective in today's environment. However, despite this recognition, very few organizations are making the necessary changes. The following sections discuss some of the most common reasons I see for this lack of change and the obstacles marketers face when seeking to transform their demand generation practice.

Lack of Patience

Several years ago my team and I were working with a large client in the payment processing sector on transforming the company's approach to demand generation. The organization had one of the leading marketing automation solutions and had invested heavily in building its own CRM system and integrating it into multiple other technologies. The company had a well-staffed marketing team and a very large, contracted sales force. The sales reps were responsible for sourcing their own leads, but it was now expected that the marketing department would carry some of the load. However, even with all of this investment and technology, the marketing department was still struggling in several areas and was even having issues simply driving traffic to the company's website. To add to the department's difficulties, the marketers had no defined buyer personas and kept missing their goals for generating leads; this led to a complete loss in confidence from the sales team. The company had also lost the confidence of their buyers; before our engagement the company had conducted some research and surveys that showed their customers' frustration with the company's lack of engagement with them. Customers found it difficult to get information and buy products. The buyer surveys revealed a very low buyer satisfaction rating. Marketing was in trouble and needed to make some drastic changes.

Our work began with a Demand Process Audit[SM], which revealed many gaps in the company's approach to demand generation. We presented these findings to organization's senior leadership team, and I recommended as a next step looking at developing a strategic demand generation pilot targeted at one key audience segment. One of the marketing directors asked for an estimated timeline for developing the strategy and then implementing the program (program implementation includes technology configuration, building the program in the marketing automation platform, website optimization, development of new content, and so on). I told him he could expect the process to take 28 to 32 weeks from start to finish, and to this he instantly responded, "That's unacceptable!" The CMO who was also in the meeting followed with "I will have to agree, we cannot wait that long to usher in a new way of doing things, we need to move faster and see change happen now. We are getting far too much pressure from the vice president of sales, and there is no way we can take this long."

Here was a severely flawed organization that agreed there were numerous gaps in its Demand Process and was therefore not performing to the needed levels in demand generation. Moreover, the company's customers were having a subpar buying experience, and the company had been operating at subpar levels for several years. However, despite the honest feedback from customers and an understanding that something drastic needed to occur, the company's marketing leaders lacked the understanding that a strategic, perpetual, buyer-centric demand generation program and moving to a transformational Demand Process approach cannot happen in a matter of weeks. We already had outlined what we could do to support the sales team as the pilot program was being built; however, because the company's marketing leaders found the timeline too long, the plan was out of the question. They wanted something quick and easy, something that they could point to as a proof for the sales department that they were doing something to address the shortcomings even though they knew that ultimately their problems required much more than a quick fix.

Change in large organizations cannot be rushed. It takes time and often the pressures put on marketers create a situation where marketing leaders feel compelled to deliver a quick fix. However, when it comes to retooling the approach to demand generation, there are no quick fixes. This is not to say that there will not be achievable, milestones along the way that do have impact, but a full transformation will take time and demands patience on the part of the organization. Understanding this at the outset of these endeavors is crucial for organizations to succeed.

Lack of Leadership

"We are seeing a new guard of internal marketing leaders evangelizing this vision," my colleague and business partner, Adam Needles, wrote. "But in delivering Demand Process Transformation initiatives to dozens of $1 billion-plus B2B organizations, it's rare I've seen the CMO lead this initiative. Too often I've seen the opposite. And—even worse—often I've found the CMO does not even fully 'get' the idea of building and optimizing Demand Process to drive perpetual revenue."[2]

I experienced this lack of leadership firsthand when I took a new role at the software company I worked for before cofounding ANNUITAS. I had previously been in a solutions marketing role, and my team had made great progress in developing a demand generation and lead management process that was contributing to pipeline and impacting revenue. As a result of this success, the CMO asked me if I would consider taking on a new role in leading a new department focused on opportunity management for the entire organization. This new role was just one of the changes and part of the significant investment the organization was making in demand generation. Seeing this as a chance to advance my career and lead a new team, I accepted the role.

The goals of my new organization were pretty straightforward:

- Establish a global process and framework to ensure that leads are routed to the right sales representatives.
- Work with sales to implement SLAs to ensure timely follow-up with qualified leads.
- Implement metrics that could show the ROI from marketing's investment.

Before we could begin implementing this new process, however, we had to gather some data that would inform the approach and the development of the global process we were charged with implementing. As part of the data gathering, interviews were conducted with various departments, including Information Technology (IT,) directors of marketing, sales managers, sales reps, channel managers, and others. We needed access to various sales and marketing systems and had to be able to pull reports from them. The intended goal was to get a clear view of the current operational construct of the organization and understand how technology was being used to enable it. We needed to find out whether we needed to start from scratch or could use and build on an already established process in one or a few areas of the company.

Less than one month into the new role, my new boss, the vice president of marketing called me and in an agitated tone asked, "What the hell are you doing? Sales and IT are pissed!" He explained that he had been getting phone calls from leaders in the sales and IT departments asking why my team was being so disruptive and why we were asking for access to systems and supporting documentation. Unfortunately, this one call derailed the entire approach to our initiative as it halted any chances of the change we were hoping to deliver. It did not matter that this was a department the CMO and vice president had helped construct, that the business desperately needed this kind of role to ensure the investments in marketing were producing satisfactory ROI. It also did not matter that with new process and approaches this initiative could have a positive impact on the bottom line. The message was clear: no changes would take place, largely because marketing lacked the necessary leadership to move the process forward.

The first point of failure of my leadership team was its lack of preparation. Unbeknownst to my team, the other departments in the organization were not to be part of the process and development of this new department; it was purely a marketing department initiative. We also discovered that the other departments had not been notified of my new department so they had no understanding of the help we needed from them to succeed. Second, at the first sign of resistance from other departmental leaders in the company, the marketing leaders driving this initiative quickly backed down and pulled their support even though they knew continuing with it would be best for the business.

If B2B marketing professionals are going to transform their approach to demand generation, changes will be required that will impact and involve more than just the marketing teams. For this change to be permanent, strong leadership is needed.

Fear of Change Leading to Acceptance of the Status Quo

- "I do not want to tie our marketing team or our efforts to revenue, that scares me to death."
- "I do not want to take on the formidable challenge of rebaking our approach to the degree necessary. It will cause too many waves in the organization."

These are statements I have heard in the past two years from marketing leaders about the need for change in their business. In all of these instances, the leaders have admitted there is a need to transform, but overall they are not ready to embark on the journey or do the work necessary to succeed. They choose instead to stay in the status quo while also expecting results to improve. In most cases I find that the real issue behind the decision of continuing with business as usual is a fear of change. Make no mistake, the enormity of what needs to happen in many B2B midsized and enterprise organizations can be daunting; strong leadership is needed to chart the course and ensure that organizations are maximizing the return on their investments in demand generation. Those who shy away from this task are not equipped to usher in the era of change that is so desperately needed.

Taking Shortcuts

There is temptation in any kind of initiative to cut some corners or take a shortcut as a way to speed up the transformation process. It is very easy for companies starting down the transformational path to fall into this trap; however, there is no shortcut to change.

We worked with one client not long ago on developing a strategic demand generation program, which uncovered seven unique personas in the buying process and delivered a very detailed insight into the buying process. As with any strategy, the goal was to have a dialogue with the buyers all along the purchase path and align the organization's people, processes, content, and technology to enable these conversations. In this particular case this meant creating 41 new pieces of content, reconfiguring the marketing automation platform, implementing a new lead qualification model and making changes to the role of the inside lead qualification team. At the end of the presentation we laid out the implementation plan, including the content needs, budget, and timeline (which was going to be 26 weeks). After much discussion over the course of several days and feedback from the company's CEO, the marketing leaders made the decision to "compress the strategy," as the vice president of marketing put it. "We want to get there, but we need to trim this down as we believe it is too complex." The program was complex because the organization served a complex audience with a long buying cycle and numerous people with differing views and roles involved in the buying cycle. Unfortunately, B2B vendors cannot tell their buyers that they want them to compress their buying decisions and make it less complex. Despite this fact, this company's leadership made the decision to roll all the personas into one; this reduced the number of pieces of content needed and the overall implementation timeline. In their minds, the content would speak to the differing needs of the seven personas, and the program could be launched in less than 12 weeks. Despite our best efforts, we were unable to change these executives' minds, and the program as well as their transition to change was an utter failure. In hindsight, we should have declined to engage any further with this client, given the executives' insistence on cutting corners. This is one lesson I learned, and I will not allow this to happen again; the process of change cannot be cut short and still be successful.

There are no shortcuts to change. As of today, the organization described above is right back where it started; it is no further along in connecting with buyers along their purchase path. It is stuck in the old way of tactical marketing.

Clearly, B2B marketing leaders must become the change agents in their organizations and empower their people to do things differently, the right way, in order to drive demand effectively and have a positive impact on their company's bottom line.

Pride of Ownership

Whatever the challenges facing marketing departments today, there is no lack of effort. And it is this effort and the pride in the hard work marketers have put into their jobs that sometimes can get in the way of transformation.

For example, my team and I were working with a client in the early stages of designing and implementing a strategic demand generation program. As is our approach with all of our clients, we were meeting with the marketing leaders for a midpoint check-in to present our findings on buyer insights, content audit, and initial thoughts regarding the buyers' journey and content architecture. As we presented the findings of the content audit, the vice president of content said, "We have so much great content, I am curious to see what you found." This was in essence a "tell" about the pride he had in the content he and his team had developed. As we went through the findings of the content audit and the initial drafts of the content architecture, which showed the gaps in the organization's content in regard to the newly discovered buyers' journey, this vice president took on a very defensive posture. At some point in the discussions he chimed in with a disagreement about our findings and recommendations. "I do not think we need to go and create all of this new content, we have plenty of content that we have invested in, and we can use it for this purpose." I explained that like many organizations, this organization indeed had a lot of content, and some of it could be used as a part of the new program. However, the existing content was largely focused on product and on the organization as a vendor; it was not focused on the buyers. The vice president replied, "It is good content; I should know, I wrote most of it." He was proud of the work, he had ownership of it, and he felt under attack and inclined to defend his position. This is quite understandable as there was a considerable amount of work being done, the content was well written, and the vice president had done a good job at spreading the word in the organization about the amount of content his team had created. However, this content was not the right content for their buyers' journey, and it would not be effective in the Engage or Nurture stages of a demand generation program.

Pride of ownership can quickly become a roadblock in many organizations. Teams working hard and doing what they believe is the right thing for their business can still have a hard time hearing that not all of their work and effort is contributing to revenue as much as they thought it would or could.

In order for transformation to be successful, the people involved must understand that not all of what has been done in the past will be effective going forward. There will be situations of people having worked hard to accomplish something, having invested effort, and being proud of the final product, a product that needs to be left behind. This does not mean that those were not worthwhile investments at that earlier time. It means that with new information, as markets and buyers change, marketers cannot expect to simply repeat what they have done year after year and expect the same positive results. Organizations seeking to advance demand generation must understand the psychology of change and stress to their people that these changes and approaches must be taken seriously, but not personally. It should be understood that change can provide individuals with opportunity to grow professionally, enhance their skills, and advance their careers. The reality is that a new approach and method will increase effectiveness, but it necessitates that egos be left out of the process and that people keep open minds.

Lack of Vision

A phrase I have heard my father say many times is "Where there is no vision, the imagination runs wild." This is true of any endeavor, especially one the magnitude of organizational transformation. In a conversation I had with Nick Panayi, head of digital marketing and global brand at Computer Sciences Corporation (CSC) about the change he has spearheaded, he stated, "My first 90 days were spent getting people to buy into the vision. I was in constant communication with each office globally, casting the vision, and getting the buy-in at every level of marketing and sales leadership as well as key support functions like IT, legal, and others. I wanted our teams to see that we could move from being a company stuck in the old way of marketing and change to a new way of demand generation that was modern and connected with our buyers. I knew we could not just start changing things, we needed to paint a vision for what could be for our people."[3]

What Nick understood and so many leaders fail to understand is that change will rarely be lasting if there is not the necessary support for it. This applies to all levels in the organization and not just to the leaders who then force changes down to the various levels of the organization. Without vision casting, people begin to make their own assumptions, become fearful of the change, and as a result, begin to resist the change or refuse to become a part of it. Leaders who want to see this new approach be permanent must take the first step of casting the vision and sharing how the new vision will impact the organization. This is hardly a one-time endeavor but should be done continually throughout the process to ensure that everyone is on the same page and moving forward together in the same direction. Some people will immediately make the mental change. Others will want to see the change in action and have it come into clear focus before they are ready to make the cognitive choice to be part of the big picture.

Political Agendas

There is little that can derail an organization's makeover as easily as people with political agendas. Many of us have been exposed to folks who take every opportunity to promote their own self-interest above that of the organizations, who undermine communications with their hallway conversations, and who may appear to be on board with decisions but cause disruption behind the scenes. This behavior is often motivated by deep-seated fear; people behaving in this way often believe that their role or position will be minimized. Having worked with many organizations through this process, I have found there are often one or two individuals in a company who allow themselves to put their own agendas ahead of what is best for the company. However, when an organization is successful, these political agendas are often diffused quickly, and the advancement of the organization becomes the focus.

For example, most recently I worked with a multinational manufacturing company that had a very politically charged environment. After working with the people there for many months and seeing that several individuals were going to great lengths to sabotage the program and advance their own agendas, I called a meeting with one of the key internal marketing leaders, our main point of contact, and one of the more disruptive individuals. The latter was going to the point of providing false information. I started the call by reminding both of why we were working together and of the ultimate goal of achieving a Demand Process state. As both individuals quickly agreed, we discussed that in working with clients, we often come across challenges and issues, and this call would be an opportunity to "mine for conflict." The whole point of this call was to call out this one individual's disruption in a direct but diplomatic way. This would expose the person and his politicking to the marketing leadership, but also get him to see that he could have a significant positive role in this transformation. Indeed, this person's involvement and cooperation were wanted and needed.

It is vital that those who are driving such a major change be aware of potentially disruptive behavior and eliminate it as soon as possible. As is to be expected, some of these disruptive individuals never make the turn and either opt out of the process by leaving the organization or must be terminated in order to keep things moving forward. These are not easy things to have occur in a company of any size, but they must be taken into account; as one industry analyst put it, "This is one of the reasons this kind of endeavor necessitates intestinal fortitude by the leaders."[4]

Not Fully Committing to the Full Extent of Change

I recently spoke with a prospect whose team was explaining to me the demand generation support team members needed and the plans they had put in place for the coming year. This organization sold financial optimization software, and the marketers wanted to design content that would speak to CFOs. They told me that they had held a workshop with their executive team and identified the key messages they wanted to deliver to CFOs, and those key messages were going to serve as the content basis for an upcoming campaign. I asked these marketers if they had validated any of these messages with their customers or prospects—they had not done so. I explained the importance of developing content that is buyer-centric and that for purchases of this size (their average sales price was greater than $300K) there would most likely be buying committees, and this would affect their content plan. I told these marketers that while CFOs would most certainly be part of that committee, it was important to identify the other key buying personas in the organization, their involvement along the purchase path, and their unique patterns of content consumption. Unfortunately, these marketers had not done any work in developing buyer personas, other than that of the CFO, and had not developed messaging for any other role in the organization. To remedy this I showed them the approach they should be taking to demand generation and how they would then achieve a better overall result. One of the individuals on the team replied, "Everything you have said makes sense, and I see the need for change and the big picture view of why it is needed. However, we want to take some incremental steps toward the change and just start with the CFO and then see if that will move things forward rather than embarking on the large change and trying to approach all of the buyers with a strategic pilot program."

Although I understood the concern, transforming demand is an all-or-nothing proposition. That is, organization leaders cannot expect to make changes to just one small area of their demand generation strategy and also expect to have any kind of substantial impact. When I explained this, the marketing executives said they would think about this, but at this stage, they were concerned about initiating any change endeavor via a pilot program and would rather just proceed incrementally. Organizations that truly want to improve how they drive demand and see the change that is needed become part of the fabric of their marketing culture cannot do change halfway. They must commit to it fully, and it is only then that they will see the benefits and overall improvements.

I speak to many marketers and have been part of several marketing organizations that have failed, for many reasons, in their endeavors to change. This should not discourage any marketing department or marketing leader to embrace change. Rather, it should serve as a warning that is important to understand what may derail this initiative in an organization and to be aware of those reasons throughout the process. Change does not necessarily come easily, but by recognizing the signs of failure and the potential roadblocks marketers can identify potential obstacles as the transformation continues.

CHAPTER 4

Action Does Not Equal Change

About two years ago, I received a call from a large multibillion dollar manufacturer who had initiated a search for a marketing automation platform. The company had spent the past year piloting a solution with an outside agency, and the executives had then concluded they wanted to adopt a global platform because that had made a big difference in how my contact's line of business performed prior to the marketing automation. When I asked about the results, she told me they were able to execute more campaigns and had succeeded in adding several thousand new names to their database. Expecting to hear more in terms of benefit and change, I probed further. But there was nothing quantifiable they could point to as a proof of success. The results they were so excited about were that they could do more, faster and easier, but there was no indication that what they were doing was any better than before.

The marketing director asked if my firm would help the company select a marketing automation system because the staff lacked experience in purchasing marketing technology. When I asked what, besides more campaigns, they wanted to accomplish with a global platform, she paused as if unsure how to answer. The marketers did not have a defined plan or strategy for maximizing the purchase and were at a loss as to how to set objectives to drive maximum revenue results. In the course of a few conversations and meetings with others in the organization, we were able to show the executives that simply having a platform would not help them improve the value of their marketing activities and would certainly not lead to any change.

Many of the B2B marketers I deal with talk about lacking the time to accomplish the tasks at hand. Recently at a marketing conference with two hundred B2B marketing professionals I asked the audience, "How many here feel they do not have enough time to do their jobs?" Over half of the attendees raised their hands. After the session, one of the attendees told me, "I was so relieved to see all of the other hands go up when you asked that question. I never feel I have enough time, and as a result I do not feel like we are doing anything well." This is the plight of many marketers as more and more actions are being taken, with little result, and the flurry of activity shows no signs of slowing down. According to multiple surveys, marketers will be doing and spending more in 2015 and even more in 2016:

- As many as 50 percent of global B2B marketers will increase their budget in 2015 with more than half of that being spent on digital initiatives.[1]
- A total of 70 percent of B2B marketing organizations are creating more content than they did in 2014.[2]
- More than 60 percent of marketing groups run more than 15 campaigns on an annual basis.[3]
- Marketers will spend more on technology as indicated by a projected industry revenue growth of 60 percent.[4]
- As many as 69 percent of marketers use between 5–10 different tactics to execute their marketing.[5]

However, despite all of this activity and spending, B2B marketing organizations are failing miserably in delivering results:

- Only 38 percent of marketing departments say they are effective with their use of content marketing.[6]
- And 58.5 percent of those who manage demand generation say they are not effective in meeting their goals.[7]
- Only 21 percent say they are effective at tracking the ROI of their content.[8]

This is a whole lot of effort and investment for very little return. Marketers need to examine the impact of these activities rather than deluding themselves into thinking that being busy is the way to achieve results or transformation.

The Importance of a Standard Approach

Developing a comprehensive plan for change is often a step many marketing leaders overlook. One client company I worked with last year saw the success of its demand generation pilot program and wanted to select two other lines of business and run two more programs. The vice president of demand generation thought that if the first pilot program was successful, just building two more and replicating the programs across the organization would make sense. What he was missing was that in order for the company to see a change and align the people, process, content, and technology with his buyers, he needed a plan, and the process would be more complex than replicating an existing strategy. Simply developing more content across various business units and different geographies was not going to bring about the changes needed in the demand generation function.

In order for organizations to apply the experience from a pilot program and ensure the Demand Process model is replicated effectively across the organization, there must be a common framework. Defining this approach is accomplished by developing a Demand Process Blueprint[SM].

Just like a homebuilder would never embark on building a home without a blueprint, organizations must realize that the only way to realize effectual change is to do the same. With the complexities of large enterprise organizations, a planned, methodical approach is needed to ensure the changes become permanent. The Blueprint ensures that the changes that were realized with a business, product line, or audience segment as a result of the program pilot are "federated" or become the standard for all demand generation programs across the entire organization. It is the process whereby the Demand Process Framework[SM] is adopted across the enterprise (see figure 4.1).

Figure 4.1   ANNUITAS Demand Process Framework.

However, unlike many frameworks that are adopted by organizations, the Blueprint also provides the flexibility needed to account for nuances throughout the organization. One example of this need for flexibility is an organization for which we were developing a Blueprint. One line of business (that accounted for approximately 30 percent of the company's total revenue) was very transactional with an average sales cycle of seven days. However, the rest of the organization had more strategic sales cycles, some lasting as long as nine months. When developing the Blueprint, we had to consider how to support both sales models and their demand generation needs, while adhering to a common standard concerning people, process, content, and technology. These kinds of complexities are not uncommon; among the variables that should be taken into consideration are also geographic differences, distribution channels (direct versus channel), personnel resources, and requirements in the particular region. Every aspect of demand generation needs to be considered in the development of a Blueprint.

What Makes Up a Blueprint?

The Blueprint is more than just a document that is developed with a checklist of items that need to be changed. The Blueprint is the document that serves as the guidebook for change. The Blueprint defines the Demand Process governance, the content marketing model, the approach to developing the conversation with the buyers, the lead management process for an organization, including the data policies, lead qualification standards, lead routing flows, and the establishment of SLAs between marketing and sales. In addition this document addresses the alignment of the marketing and sales teams as well as e-mail governance; it also sets forth how technology will be managed and what standard KPIs will measure demand generation performance across the enterprise. All of this must be defined on a corporate, global basis to ensure consistency and standardization of demand generation across the organization.

As with any initiative, the Blueprint must be developed with the buyer in mind. A Blueprint defines the multiple segments of buyers the organization targets. Companies vary widely in this; I have worked with companies that have four unique buyer segments and those that have fifteen. Some organizations base their marketing on a vertical target market; others on title and some on a solution set. However, identifying the unique buying segments that your company serves allows you to see how the rest of the processes can support the interaction with these buyers and how many individual buyer-focused demand generation programs you need to develop and implement.

Demand Generation Center of Excellence

The Blueprint also serves to define the structure of a new organization. As mentioned earlier, it is not uncommon for organizations to have their marketing departments set up in a silo structure, organizing departments either by tactics, function, or lines of business. These structures do not provide a collaborative or cohesive approach to interacting with buyers. To remedy this, demand generation needs to be a department of its own. When working with our clients we call this department a Demand Generation Center of Excellence[SM] (DGCoE). This model allows organizations to build one department that is responsible to the various demand generation functions and can fully focus on delivering strategic, perpetual demand generation programs.

The development and setup of a DGCoE is perhaps one of the biggest changes that will occur in an organization, as this is where leadership and people are impacted the most. As the plans come into focus and organizations move from a tactical to a buyer-centric approach to demand generation, traditional marketing roles are often changed and sometimes even eliminated. While this will be challenging, organizations must reconfigure their teams because if they do not take the steps to build up a full DGCoE, they will not realize the full benefit of dedicated resources focused on generating demand.

My team and I worked with a global enterprise software company on developing a Demand Process Blueprint; as part of this assignment, we outlined the construction of a DGCoE model. The organizational structure was very fractured as they had a vice president of demand generation, but the execution of demand generation activities was distributed across several regions and various departments with no uniform approach guiding them. Most of the directives were coming from the sales team. It was commonplace for a sales group to ask the marketing team for a campaign to a certain audience or for a local event and expect that the marketing team would support those requests. There was no clear process or definition of what demand generation was in the organization, and rather than using a proactive approach, the marketing department was reactive and consequently not producing the desired results.

The DGCoE model we proposed addressed these issues and was designed to ensure global alignment with the buyer segments (which also would support sales) as well as region/field support. Our model provided standardization and ensured a more strategic, buyer-centric, programmatic approach to demand generation. Implementing the DGCoE necessitated some big changes within the organization, but in the long term it would give the company much better coverage and produce better results. Several weeks after presenting the model, the organization showed us a new model of their own, which only partially incorporated some of what we had delivered, but also included remnants of the previous standard process of sales dictating marketing's focus. Unfortunately, the company's model only went half-way; our client focused on executing the tactics of demand generation and failed to make the new demand generation process fully focused on the buyers. Instead, many of the decisions regarding demand generation were still left in the hands of the sales department. As we discussed the merits of the company's proposed model and pointed out that it would not change the fact that marketing decisions were based on requests from the sales team, the heads of marketing said, "Your model was too big of a change for us, and at this point we cannot afford to have this big of a shift with sales. We will make the changes incrementally and eventually get to a fully focused demand generation model." We have all heard the expression, "no pain, no gain." In this case this was absolutely true; a big change was exactly what the company needed. Organizations that succeed in their quest for transformation make the needed changes no matter how difficult they may seem; they don't stop at just some of the needed changes.

Often, I am asked how to construct a department like the DGCoE according to the buyers' purchase path. One client, after detailing the intricate steps the company's buyers take to purchase, asked, "How do we build an organization to cover that?" She was concerned that to build an organization that aligns with the every stage of the purchase path would be virtually impossible. Trying to build an organization that maps to every potential step in the buying process would indeed be impossible; however, a DGCoE should be align with the macro stages of Engage, Nurture, and Convert. As Convert happens primarily via the sales team, the two main stages a DGCoE should support are Engagement and Nurturing. This is not to say demand generation will not play an active role in supporting and developing content for the convert stage, but the primary focus of the DGCoE will be on the Engage and Nurture stages of the buying cycle; this is where marketing has the most control.

One of our clients had a content team that was responsible for creating all of the demand generation content in the organization, and the content managers were responsible and aligned to specific vertical markets. In working with them to construct their DGCoE model, we identified that the content team was not aligned to the company's buyers. To address this, we divided the team into Engagement content specialists and Nurture content specialists. We grouped people in this way because the content in the Engage stage differs fundamentally from that in the Nurture stage in form and tone. This requires those developing the content to focus on each particular stage rather than be content generalists. In this new model, these Engagement and Nurture content specialists report to the manager of a global demand generation program; this manager was responsible for the development of the buyer-centric, strategic demand generation program as well as for the implementation of that program(s). This alignment with one program manager overseeing the entire program strategy and implementation and having content and processes that mapped to the buyers' journey has had a significant impact on the company's overall program results and allowed it to have an improved dialogue with buyers; at the same time, the company has established a common company-wide framework for demand generation.

The other hallmark of a DGCoE that makes it so effective is that it is distributed across the enterprise. I see organizations trying to compartmentalize their marketing with a small group of people who manage various functions in one geographic location; they also try to manage the marketing automation technology with a group of "power users" and other tactical teams. However, this setup limits the organization's ability to have a standardized process allowing global programs. In contrast, high-performing sales organizations have established a process all the sales people follow. In addition, in such organizations each sales representative is given access to the CRM (customer relationship management) system to keep track of interactions with the respective prospects and to manage forecasts. Imagine if each time sales representatives wanted to update a record, record a deal, or add notes to a prospect record in the company's CRM tool, they had to send a request to a centralized team to have it done for them. The logjam, lack of transparency, and failures in execution would quickly become unmanageable. Yet, this is what many CMOs require of their marketing teams when they decide to "compartmentalize" the demand generation and marketing automation function with a small group of individuals in charge.

For example, one global services organization that had numerous lines of business and solutions had built a global demand generation team that was centrally located at the company's West Coast office. This team was responsible for defining the strategy and developing the content; it also included a small group of marketing automation power users who were responsible for executing the (tactical) campaigns globally. As part of its campaign process, the team created a "campaign guidebook" that was then distributed globally to inform the other regions about the campaigns. After receiving feedback from the regions, the centralized team then would develop the campaign assets and then hand the campaign off to the team of marketing automation power users, who would begin to build and execute the campaigns. With this approach, the process quickly began to erode. The various regions, despite providing constructive feedback to the marketing team, began to push back against the campaigns being developed because people in the global regions felt the campaigns were too North American focused because the core themes and messages were developed by the North American team. In response to this, teams in the various regions began creating their own plans and programs to give the program a regional and local flavor. Moreover, the marketing automation power users were unable to keep up with the demand of the influx of so many tactical campaigns. Once again, in order to accomplish what was needed in other geographies and regions the regional teams either hired outside agencies to run their campaigns or purchased other marketing automation solutions to have more direct control and meet their deadlines. Eventually, this led to a very fractured and frustrated organization that lacked the proper governance and standards and was moving further away from delivering ongoing strategic programs. One of the company's directors told me the demand generation operation had the feel of the "wild, wild west," with everyone launching campaigns with different standards, objectives, and tactics.

Constructing an organization that is distributed yet coordinated and allows different regions to be part of a global program—that is, to execute the program regionally while adhering to a common standard—is what organizations aiming to grow demand effectively need to do. Of course, this will be a big change from what is in place at many companies, but the improved results will be worth the effort.

The Core Principles of a Blueprint

As an organization seeks to develop its own unique blueprint, there are several core principles necessary for it to have an impact. The first principle is the understanding that *all* demand generation content, regardless of what channel it is developed for, must be aligned to the buying process. This puts an end to the idea of a one-and-done campaign approach and instead shifts thinking to a continual "what's next" in terms of developing a conversation with buyers. All the content developed for every program needs to be designed to advance the dialogue with buyers; otherwise the content is unnecessary. Beyond the content, the Blueprint seeks to define all people, processes, and technology that support demand generation from the perspective of buyers and their approach to purchasing.

The second core principle is the necessity to ensure that lead nurturing is a holistic part of any program (not a separate activity) and serves both to educate and to qualify buyers along their purchase journey. This ensures that buyers are always engaged in a dialogue and interacting with content, rather than being sent to the sales team before they are ready to have that sales conversation.

Lastly, the Blueprint provides structure for an e-mail cadence that eliminates the spam effect so many buyers feel. Several years ago, a colleague and I conducted an audit for a large enterprise security and antivirus company. We discovered that an unusually high number of customers and prospects had opted out of the e-mail communication. As we investigated further, we found that the organization had no documented rationale or even a schedule for sending e-mail; it was truly a batch and blast scenario. Unfortunately, as a result, some contacts received two and sometimes three e-mails in a given day. In reviewing the e-mail data, we found that one customer who had opted out had received well over 300 e-mails from the company in one year. The lack of a documented rationale had a significant impact on the company's e-mail deliverability scores and its ability to service its customers. For that company, e-mail was the main channel for alerting its customers about suspected viruses and phishing schemes. Many of the firm's customers had opted out or blocked the organization's e-mails so as not to be bothered anymore by sales and marketing messages. However, as a result, those customers were missing out on critical information they needed to be protected against online threats and to protect their networks. Establishing a defined e-mail cadence and a clear approach to communication determined by interactions with buyers and their place in the purchase process is a key component of any blueprint.

Leading change that impacts people, processes, content, and technology across an organization is no small task and takes careful planning. Simply trying to drive change, without guidance or a documented approach, will only lead to change for the sake of change and will most likely not be permanent. As one marketing professional said "We make changes, hope they work, and then we wait a few months and change again."

The planning and development of a blueprint is necessary for any significant and lasting change as it allows an organization to stay on course and not be distracted in the all important process of transforming the demand generation process.

CHAPTER 5

Changing the Marketing and Sales Mind-set

Much as marketing departments need to change and adapt the approach to demand generation, the necessary changes do not stop there. Among others, sales departments also need to adapt to the changes in the B2B ecosystem. Given the incredible shifts that have occurred in the B2B landscape in the past several years, this change needed at the sales level has never been more urgent than it is today. When I began my career in marketing, my role was primarily focused on "sales enablement," which at that time meant ensuring that the sales teams had what they needed to perform their jobs effectively. This included the delivering templates, data sheets, white papers, and supporting field events. Today marketing's role is much different and more strategic; yet, I continue to see organizations where the sales teams fail to understand how the B2B buying landscape has changed and how they need to work collaboratively with the marketing teams in order to have more success in connecting with more sophisticated buyers. Many sales teams want to continue with outdated approaches and ineffective methodologies; while sufficient 10 to 15 years ago, these methodologies no longer work today.

For instance, recently I met with a client who was headquartered in Europe and had recently expanded and established operations in the United States. The company sold application development solutions to various levels of IT operations, and we were working together to develop an end-to-end strategic demand generation program. At that meeting I presented the details of the purchase journey the company's buyers went through to purchase its solutions. This firm had traditionally called contacts as soon as they filled out a form (in an attempt to get the contact to agree to a demo), and if successful, the contact would be passed on quickly to the sales department as a lead. Not surprisingly, a majority of what the firm's marketers called leads (which were really inquiries) and passed onto sales were low-quality prospects and the sales department was wasting time following up with these leads and as a result was struggling to meet quota. We were brought in to develop a strategic, buyer-centric approach, and one of the anticipated results was higher quality leads for the sales team. I was halfway through presenting the journey the company's buyers take to purchase, when the vice president of sales broke in and said, "I am not too concerned with what our buyers do to buy our products. What I and my sales team are looking to do is disrupt that purchase path and ensure we are closing those deals." Clearly, he had not embraced the idea of a new process and failed to understand the different approach buyers take to purchases today. I asked him why he was so certain that sales reps could indeed succeed with this "disruptive approach," and he responded, "I've been in sales for 20 years; I think I know how to sell."

What he failed to understand is that although successful in the past, the role of sales has changed dramatically over the years. Buyers are no longer dependent on a sales guy or sales teams to provide product information; in fact, they manage and execute much of their own buying process, especially in the early stages, without any help from a vendor. However, this manager was unwilling to change his approach.

While it would be easy to blame sales teams for not wanting to change and to keep their place on the corporate throne, I am not sure that many marketing organizations have given sales teams the confidence that they are capable of leading in this new approach to connecting with contemporary buyers. Marketing executives often tell me that "our company has always been a 'sales-led' organization." Of course it has. Sales drive revenue and the importance of sales departments should never be diminished; they are the revenue engine of any organization. However, many marketing leaders are using this as an excuse to not lead the necessary change. The changes that have occurred in the B2B marketplace call for marketing and sales departments to lead together.

In all the articles, workshops, speeches, and webinars I have seen about the need for marketing to change, I have rarely seen or heard anyone speak about the need for B2B sales to do the same. Once I mentioned this issue to an industry analyst who stated, "Sales does need new skills for this modern B2B buying approach, but they are further behind than marketing."[1] She is absolutely right and what we need is for marketing departments to be the catalyst in helping sales departments change, and both sides of the organization must be in sync.

In 2001 I joined McAfee (now part of Intel) as a lead generation manager for a specific line of business. My first day in that position was the first day of the global sales kickoff, and I was eager to jump right in, learn more about the organization, and use this as a springboard for getting to know the sales teams I would be working with. During my lunch break I made it a point to find the vice president of the West and his sales team to introduce myself. After brief introductions, the vice president turned to me and said, "Carlos, I am going to be honest with you, I have been here for a long time, and not once have I seen marketing do anything for me and so while I welcome you to the company, I do not hold out much hope that you will be any different."

If that is not a wake-up call, I don't know what is. Rather than be defeated by his remark, I took it as a challenge to change his mind about marketing and to better understand what I could do as the manager of lead generation to change his mind. Over the next few weeks I found out that he was right about one thing: in the past the marketing department had not done anything to help his team in terms of generating quality leads. The next time we met, I asked him and his counterpart in the East if we could go to dinner. At the dinner I recalled our conversation and told him he was right in his past assessment of marketing and proceeded to apologize on behalf of the marketing department that the sales team was in such a position. I then asked them what they needed to achieve their goals and whether they would commit to support my team in making the changes necessary to get them what they needed. I made sure they understood that not all the changes required were on the marketing side;

we needed the sales teams to make some changes as well to move things forward. We also needed sales teams to understand that things would not change fundamentally within a span of two or three weeks, but if we worked together, we could align and see better results. At the end of that dinner, both men understood that our goal was to work together and end what had traditionally been an adversarial relationship.

I was delighted that the following year that same vice president who a year earlier had told me he had no expectations for marketing, stood on stage at the sales kick-off and asked his sales team to applaud the marketing effort. What had changed? How did we get the sales force to adopt a different mind-set and agree to work together with the marketing department rather than against it? The first step was admitting that marketing was part of the problem and also pointing out that in order to fix the problem, there would need to be trade-offs as well as challenges for both sides.

Changing the mind-set of sales team members can be accomplished. In my experience at McAfee and in working with other clients, this meant that at times the marketing people have to educate and teach the sales force some of the new approaches taken in marketing. For example, at times we had to tell the sales teams we were going to stop investing in certain activities they had become accustomed to (golf days, field events, trade shows, etc.) because they were not producing the expected revenue in the long run and therefore had no value in terms of demand generation. As with any change, there were bumps in the road, but for the first time in the organization the marketing department was leading, and sales, as a result of the groundwork laid at the leadership level, was following.

Many marketing and sales teams fail to change their mind-set because they settle back into traditional roles and just accept that this is the way it is. At a marketing conference in Denver last year I was able to take some questions after my speech. One of the attendees asked, "I have been trying to change the marketing approach and become more buyer-aligned for the last two years. However, the CEO leads sales and does not see the need for change, what can I do?" I told her to look for a new job. When I said that there was some laughter from the crowd, but I was dead serious and would give the same advice today. When you are in an organization where the sales leadership is unwilling to change and adapt the traditional approach so as to drive more effective demand generation, then it is time to seek out new employment rather than continue to waste time and effort.

Moving From Mind-Set to Alignment

It is one thing to get sales people to understand the new world of B2B demand generation and the new approach taken by buyers, but it is another thing entirely to create a strategic and working partnership between marketing and sales departments so that changes will actually occur. Many marketing and sales leaders tell me about the lengths they have gone to in their organizations to try and get marketing and sales forces to align, but yet that alignment seems elusive. The first step, as just discussed, is adjusting the mind-set, the second step is defining common objectives to enable alignment, and this is where marketing and sales departments often differ.

Too often marketing and sales teams have differing objectives and means of measurement. What marketing deems as valuable has no value to sales executives and vice versa. While both groups will track performance metrics for their own purposes, there should be common metrics both groups agree to in order to build a better alliance. When I was the director of marketing for a global software company, we established "marketing quotas" for sales accepted leads—leads accepted by the sales team—and began to track and manage marketing's contribution to pipeline and revenue. This was the first step in managing to metrics that mattered to sales. Over time, we were able to expand the measurements and met regularly with the sales teams to agree on the number of qualified leads that were needed to attain quota and that my marketing team would be measured against. The attainment of these quotas became part of the bonus compensation of my marketing team, as it seemed only fair that we got paid on quota attainment just as the sales team did. These new measurements gave way to marketing and sales working cohesively to drive demand and jointly measuring the results. By having these common objectives and measurements the sales and marketing alignment improved significantly, and the results were seen on the bottom line. There is marginal progress being made in B2B organizations in this area, but there is much room for improvement as only 38 percent of B2B marketing departments today have both lead and revenue quota goals.[2]

The Buyer Is King

As important as it is to have a common set of goals, the quickest way to alignment is to focus on the buyers. One persistent idea that will quickly derail any alignment between the two groups is that "sales is marketing's customer." This belief is unfortunate and only serves to widen the divide between the two organizations without leading to results that improve revenue. Sales are not marketing customers; buyers are both departments' customers.

When marketing and sales both have a clear picture of their customers and are working together to connect with their buyers in a relevant, meaningful interaction, the likelihood of alignment increases significantly. However, many marketing organizations are still not taking the necessary steps to unify their relationship with the sales teams. Only 21.7 percent of B2B marketers say that sales is very involved in the development of demand generation strategies, and less than 42 percent regularly include sales in the development of buyer personas.[3]

Recently, my team was working with a client on the development of a strategic demand generation program; the company has a successful 100-year history in industrial printing. Over the past few years, the firm's leaders have focused on their technology solutions, and while staying true to their 100-year foundation, they have made some significant changes in their product portfolio to evolve their business. They have undergone their own organizational change on many levels. Given the company's long history, many of the sales reps have long tenures and know many in the industry; they had grown accustomed to the old way of selling where the vendor drives the transaction. Our engagement began with a two-day kickoff meeting at the client's corporate headquarters in Dayton, Ohio. One of the key participants in that meeting was the Director of Sales for the product line that would be piloted. He was a very willing and active participant, and during one of the early breaks in the agenda,

I thanked him for being part of the meeting and added that I hoped he would continue to be a part of the process throughout the strategy phase and into development. He responded that "this is too important not to be here. If we [marketing and sales] cannot work together and drive toward a common purpose of understanding our buyer, then we have bigger problems. Being here and having all of us together figuring out how to better interact and sell to our buyers, that is something I will always give my time to." He was one of few in sales who understood that the marketing department was an ally in helping his team have better interactions with buyers, and he understood the strategic role demand generation needed to play. He also knew that the only way his company was going to succeed in generating demand was when both marketing and sales focused on the buyers.

The New Sales Enablement = Education

As stated earlier, demand generation is a marketing *and* sales activity; however, this is often missed. In the above case of my client, there was a collaborative and unified approach in the development of strategies with the marketing department gaining insight into buyers from a sales perspective. The Conversion stage of a demand generation program is the stage where sales reps are actively involved and conversing directly with buyers. Thus, it is vital that the sales teams understand the details of the marketing program and that the marketing department delivers the relevant content needed to enable sales teams to close the sale. This is more than just delivering a cheat sheet for sales to read from but means covering all aspects of the program, from the content that has been developed to use cases of how buyers will progress through the program and content consumption scenarios to educating the larger sales team about the qualification and scoring model. This also means enabling sales teams to use technology more effectively to manage their leads and also giving them detailed insights into who their buyers are and the conversations their buyers will want to have. Ultimately, the goal is to ensure that buyers have a seamless, cohesive buying experience; to that end there must be continuity in the dialogue as buyers move from a more self-driven, digital interaction to a live, person-to-person conversation. Marketing owns this task. While the sales department will be involved in the development of strategies and will also provide insight into buyers, this is most commonly done by a representative(s) of the sales team. These persons serve as evangelists in their organizations but are not expected to provide the full training needed for the sales teams. This training or educating is also not a one-time event; to be effective, it should be ongoing. As any program should continually be optimized, marketing needs to continually inform sales about the program's overall performance, get feedback from sales on the quality of leads, and educate sales teams on any changes that have been made to the program as a result of the optimization. These meetings should take place on a quarterly basis and will serve not only to further educate sales teams, but also go a long way toward building a collaborative approach to demand generation in the company.

Social Selling Is Not Change

One of the buzzwords in B2B selling today is social selling. Social selling is "about sales people building a strong personal brand. It is about understanding the role of content and how content can be used to tell a powerful and emotional story. And it is about growing your social connections."[4] While salespeople should still endeavor to build strong relationships with their buyers, many sales people are simply using social tools to sell in a tactical manner. I receive on average three to four solicitations each day through LinkedIn, Twitter, and other social channels from salespeople promoting their services, asking for a meeting, or imploring me to detail my purchase timeline. What they are doing is circumventing the way buyers buy today by using these social tools. One of the biggest shifts necessary for B2B sales professionals is to understand how to use these tools effectively to build relationships much the same way marketers have had to learn how to build effective content that Engages, Nurtures, and then Converts. Sales reps need to become students of their buyers and experts in the field in which they work.

For example, I was speaking about this topic in a meeting with one of our clients when one sales rep, who was very active in social media, said he could easily speak about his industry and help inform and educate his buyers. I asked him to speak to me as if he were speaking to a prospect and educate me on some industry trends without mentioning his company or any of its products. As he began to speak I looked at my watch, and after only 12 seconds he began speaking about the product he sells. With a smile he said, "That is harder than it sounds." It is indeed, but it is a skill that B2B sales reps must master whether communicating in person, via e-mail, or socially. Given that demand generation is about educating in addition to qualifying, it is vital that sales teams become proficient in the use of social media and in this way help add value to their buyers; it is essential that the content being generated helps enable buyers to proceed on their journey to purchase.

As important as it is for marketing departments to connect with their sales counterparts, success also depends on marketing integrating with other departments.

Managing the CEO Relationship

Perhaps the most important relationship CMOs need to manage is that with their CEOs. This may seem painfully obvious; however, most CMOs have a rather fragile relationship with the CEO. The Fournaise Marketing Group, one of the leading marketing measurement and management firms, conducted a study in 2012 that showed 80 percent of CEOs do not really trust their CMOs.[5] In this particular study the lack of trust is tied to CEOs being concerned that CMOs are not focusing on the "financial realities of the business." However, I often find that the reason for this disconnect is that CMOs do not have a full understanding of the overall goals and objectives of the business, and as a result, they run marketing as separate business of its own.

For example, I asked one CMO how the marketing and demand generation plans supported the corporate goals and growth objectives. She replied, "I am not clear on what the organization's goals are, but I have laid out what I expect of the marketing team and believe we will be able to achieve these in the coming year." While defining goals for the marketing department is a good step for the CMO, these goals are not effective if there is no alignment or basic understanding of how they help accomplish the corporate goals.

McKinsey & Company highlighted the importance of the CMO working with the CEO in an interview with Bert van Meurs, senior vice president of marketing for Phillips Healthcare. He described the company-wide approach Phillips Healthcare takes in marketing: "The key to a good CEO-CMO relationship is a common belief in and commitment to a common vision. If there's not this synergy between the CEO and the CMO, then the relationship won't work." He explained further, "This is my advice to new CMOs: For the first hundred days, engage and embrace the vision and make a very strong commitment on the direction. Then be an ambassador for the vision, not just to your team but to the whole organization."[6] And this is where most CMOs are missing the mark, and as a result they are not focusing on the financial realities of the business.

If CMOs are going to be change catalysts in their organizations and lead the necessary transformation, the first and most important relationship they need to forge is the one with their CEO.

A Focus on the CIO

One of the fallacies in the early days of marketing automation was that marketers could adopt this technology without involvement of IT. While marketing teams are purchasing more technology than ever before, the idea that they can implement on their own and go rogue without guidance from their IT organization is simply not reasonable. What started with marketing automation has now turned into an entire marketing technology ecosystem. Learning how these solutions integrate and link together in order to get meaningful insights into buyers is imperative to driving demand. However, this goes beyond the skills or mandate of a marketing department. In a 2013 report published by Accenture about the gap that currently exists between CMOs and CIOs we find the following statement: "Only 1 in 10 marketing and IT executives say collaboration is at the right level."[7] One of the overriding reasons for this, according to the study, is the CMOs' perception that IT is an "execution and delivery arm" of the business rather than a strategic partner. As a result, only 44 percent of CMOs see a need for collaboration with their CIOs.[8] What CMOs need to understand is that though part of IT's mission is to execute and deliver, the department's experience in optimizing technology is as important to the customer experience as any marketing tactic. Given that so much of the buying process is now digital, technologies cannot simply be cobbled together in the hopes that they will produce results.

The Information Technology Services Marketing Association (ITSMA) discussed the increase in marketing technology in a report published in 2013. It showed that despite the increase in marketing technology purchases only 30 percent of companies answered positively in terms of receiving value, and less than 30 percent of *these* rated themselves as best-in-class when it came to the use of their technology purchases.[9] When ITSMA asked about the top barriers to marketing technology success, the response list included inefficient process, no strategy or plan, and lack of governance. These are all areas where IT has immense experience. When comparing these laggard companies to those that are collaborating with their technology departments, the collaborators are outperforming the others in the following five categories:

- Targeting customers
- Contributing to revenue growth
- Generating leads
- Achieving target or exceeding campaign ROI
- Measuring campaign ROI

While 79 percent of CMOs expect the level of marketing complexity will grow over the next five years, only 48 percent feel prepared for it. This is the reason why a tighter bond between the CMO and CIO must be established.

The CFO Relationship

One area of the business where marketers have slightly improved collaboration is their relationship with the CFO. Currently, 77 percent of CMOS and 76 percent of CFOs believe that alignment between the two groups is important.[10] However, a report by Active International shows that CMOs and CFOs also differ regarding the areas that need collaboration. Currently, one of the most challenging aspects facing demand generators is the ability to demonstrate ROI; only 12 percent of CFOs rank their CMOs as excellent at "connecting marketing initiatives to ROI."[11] Besides their lack of experience in the management and integration of technologies, most B2B marketers also do not possess the skills and are not experienced in the management of proving business value. Therefore, it makes sense that marketers would aim for a tighter collaboration with their finance counterparts to demonstrate their value. The latest figures show that marketing organizations that have forged an alliance with their CFOs outperform those that have not by 35 percent.[12] This is a significant advantage, and CMOs need to work hard at improving the collaboration with their CFO counterparts.

Working with Human Resources

The organizational changes that will occur in a B2B marketing department in order to establish a dedicated demand generation team require the involvement of the human resources department. For example, when I initiated an engagement with a global enterprise software organization, the senior vice president of demand generation asked me to spend time talking to his counterpart from Human Resources (HR). He explained he knew the changes were coming and even though he had met with the head of HR and outlined the goals and objectives of our engagement, he wanted me to speak with that person to further expand the vision and "get him on board." It was great insight on his part and has enabled him to make the necessary changes needed to build a more effective demand generation team. While this relationship may not be as vital as the one between IT and the finance department, it is a relationship that should not be ignored as it will pave the way to needed personnel changes.

Successfully driving demand amidst growing complexity requires that CMOs collaborate with their C-level counterparts and do not stop at integrating with the sales department. Best-in-class organizations speak a common language, have common goals, and have the commitment to work for the growth of the business. For demand generation to be successful, the CMO needs to adopt the same mind-set.

CHAPTER 6

Aligning Content to Your Buyer

"I see and hear all the time from reading industry blogs, listening to speakers like yourself, and other articles that I need to align content to the buyers' purchase path, but nobody seems to tell me how to do that or what that really means." This is what was said to me recently in a conversation I had with a B2B marketing professional, and he was right. There has been a lot of talk about "what you need to do with content" and very little about "here is how you do it." That conversation helped me understand the reality that many marketers have not yet fully grasped this concept, and more important, have never been taught what it means to align content to the buyers' journey and how to do it.

According to CEB, vendors today only achieve 12 percent mind share with their buyers throughout the entire purchase process.[1] There are many reasons for this lack of mindshare, but I believe one of the causes is that many B2B organizations fail to have a meaningful dialogue with their buyers. What is meaningful dialogue? Think about the number of people you have met in your lifetime. These could be people you have met on an airplane, through work, or even while dining in a restaurant. I would bet that the people you remember most vividly are the ones you had a meaningful conversation with, that is, more than just the usual small talk of "Where are you headed?" or "Looks like the weather is about to turn." As vendors look to develop relevant content that aligns to their buyers, establishing a meaningful dialogue has to be the goal. Otherwise, the content is forgettable and the vendors may be as well. Therefore, this dialogue must be planned and documented in order to have a cohesive demand generation content strategy.

Defining Content

Content marketing has been a priority of B2B marketing for the past few years. Many marketing departments are establishing roles specifically focused on content development, and more money is being spent on content marketing this year (2015) than ever before. However, in my experience many marketers have not yet defined what content marketing means to their organization and how it impacts their day-to-day functions. According to the Content Marketing Institute's definition, content marketing is

> a strategic marketing approach focused on creating and distributing valuable, relevant, and consistent content to attract and retain a clearly defined audience—and, ultimately, to drive profitable customer action.[2]

In general I agree with this definition, but it must be refined further when applied to demand generation. The purpose of content in the practice of demand generation is to create an ongoing dialogue or a one-to-one interaction between a buyer and vendor. This core understanding of developing a conversation via content is necessary as it will guide the content strategy for any demand generation program.

Creating a Dialogue

Once buyers begin their buying process (in a moment also known as a trigger event), they begin searching for a solution to their challenges or problems. Trigger events can be anything from the organization needing to update its IT systems, procurement looking for a new vendor, or firms seeking cost savings opportunities, outgrowing a current vendor, complying with new industry regulations, adapting to a merger, or simply needing additional services or products to grow their business. In any case, this trigger event is where the demand generation dialogue with a buyer begins because this is where buyers become active in their buying process. Following the trigger event, buyers go through a sequence of discrete stages (information requests) throughout the purchase process; this is called the Buyer Dialogue Logic^{SM}. Understanding and documenting the intricacies of these requests will allow marketers to have content created specifically for use at the Engage, Nurture, and Convert stages of the buying process.

Currently, fewer than 29 percent of organizations align their content to each stage of the buyers' journey.[3] This lack of content alignment is due to the fact that many marketing departments are simply creating content for content's sake, rather than basing it on an understanding of the intricacies of the buying process. Although choosing this easier alternative is understandable, this leads to a very scattered conversation between buyers and vendors, which will often turn buyers off to any further engagement. In order for demand generation content to be effective, the details of the buying process must be understood; then the content can flow in a way that makes sense to the buyer and fosters an ongoing conversation.

The best way organizations can get this level of detail and begin to develop the Buyer Dialogue Logic is to interview their buyers (customers as well as those not yet customers) and get a close look at their buying process from beginning to end. The insights that marketing and sales teams have regarding buyers should also be considered as each team has good data and information about the buyers. However, these insights simply cannot replace information gathered directly from the buyers themselves. Interviews will uncover buyers' unique perspective, allowing for follow-up questions to probe for deeper explanations. In addition, speaking directly to customers and prospects gives marketers an unvarnished view of the purchase process and allows them to see through their eyes, so to speak; this simply is not possible in any other way.

Very rarely do B2B buyers begin searching the Internet or asking advice from colleagues with a product name in mind; rather, they begin their search looking for an answer or a solution to address their problems. In most buyer interviews I have conducted, buyers report going to Google^{TM}

and typing in key phrases or terms as a way to initiate the buying process. At a meeting with a demand generation team for a global health care organization, team members explained their keyword strategy and showed me the metrics they had been tracking. These marketers had been pressured by their sales and product teams to invest more in the company's product names as part of their pay-per-click (PPC) strategy. The team leader told me, "We have to continually educate our sales and product teams that prospects are not searching for our products by name. They are looking for solutions to their present challenges." He then pointed to the line in the metrics dashboard that showed the company's new product name and the number of searches conducted on that particular name, amounting to a total of ten. "You see that?" he said. "All of those searches are from our employees, not one of those searches led to a visit to our website from a prospect." This was information he was going to use to further educate the team members about how buyers buy and what they look for in their initial steps of the buying process. Understanding the trigger event that initiates a buying process and then planning the conversation that will take place next is the first step in aligning demand generation content to the buying process.

The Buying Process

Once the Buyer Dialogue Logic has been established, it is important to understand the discrete steps that buyers (keep in mind that in most B2B buying processes there are multiple buyers) take in the course of the buying process. This is the micro view versus the macro view of the Engage, Nurture, and Convert stages. Uncovering the steps in the purchase process goes far beyond the standard subdivision into interest, consensus, evaluation, and decision that many organizations use and also goes beyond the traditional linear sales funnel. Instead, the interview process leads to a step-by-step view of the buyers' path to purchase, and this will guide the development of content along the way thanks to the unique insight into the buyers' state of mind. We took this approach at ANNUITAS when we began developing our strategic demand generation program (see figure 6.1).

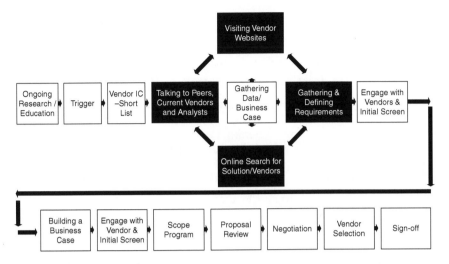

Figure 6.1 Buying Path Analysis.

We found that buyers take 12 discrete steps when looking to make a purchase for demand generation strategy services. We also learned that in the early stages of the process, as indicated by the black boxes, there was ongoing activity with buyers visiting our website, talking to peers, gathering information from industry blogs, and continually doing online searches (at times for up to a month) after they had made initial contact with us. This insight was particularly helpful because it shaped the kind of content we developed; the insight led to a clearer vision of the kind of content we needed on our website and also shaped the messages we were going to put out into the market via industry influencers.

Aligning the model of the buyers' purchase path to the buyer dialogue logic allows an organization to ensure that its conversation with buyers is relevant and meets their needs. Approaching demand generation content in this way is a transformation in itself as many organizations start with their product and service and put the buyers' needs second. I receive on average three to five e-mails per week from vendors pushing their products or services. Many of the e-mails ask if I could spare 15–30 minutes of my time to view a demo to see why I am in need of their company's product or service. This is not buyer-aligned content, and those e-mails quickly find their way to the junk folder and do nothing to endear their brand to me. Buyers want content that educates them and enables them to make a more informed purchase. According to DemandGen Report, 65 percent of B2B buyers strongly recommend that vendors "curb the sales messaging" while another 32 percent "somewhat agree" with that sentiment.[4] When developing content, the buyer has to be the focal point; this is the only way to ensure continued relevance.

The Role of Individual Personas in the Buying Process

Defining the steps of the path buyers take to purchase is just the beginning in aligning content to buyers. On average, in B2B purchases, five buyers are involved in the buying process;[5] yet, very few marketers understand what role each of these personas play throughout the process. Currently, only 33 percent of organizations take buying committees into account when creating demand generation personas.[6]

For example, my team and I developed a demand generation program for the financial services software of a large enterprise software vendor. As part of our standard process, we conducted research into the financial services market and conducted numerous interviews with the company's customers as well as with non-customers, channel partners, and marketing and sales people. When interviewing the sales reps and channel partners, we consistently heard that it was vital for them to get to the CFO to "sell" their solution. Many of the reps we interviewed expressed frustration about not being able to secure meetings with CFOs or about not receiving leads that enabled them to sell at a higher level in the organization. They believed getting to the C-suite was important because they had a high-level message specifically for the CFO whom they had identified as the key decision maker. However, our research and feedback from the interviews told a different story. Though CFOs were indeed part of the process and often initiated the buying process, they then delegated the process to the finance directors and controllers in their company and the people in these roles did the research and vendor evaluations. Only when buyers had identified a short list of two or three vendors would the CFOs get involved again and review the information their teams had prepared and make a final decision. So many sales reps wanted time with the CFOs, but their real target should have been the organizations' finance directors and controllers.

The CIO and his technology staff were also key in the buying process because they needed to approve any new technology to ensure it could be integrated into the organization's current technology stack. This CIO persona was largely overlooked in many of the interviews we had with our client's sales reps. However, this was a critical element because the CIOs were one of the key stakeholders in the purchase process and could easily stop any deal. Moreover, our research in Europe uncovered that many European companies hire individuals or small consulting companies to lead the entire purchase process and make a final recommendation. This was unique to Europe, but it was a key factor both the marketing and sales departments had to understand because a few people in the marketing organization had already recommended that leads with the title of consultant should be disqualified. The information we collected by interviewing customers directly, conducting research, and mapping out the role of each of these personas in the buying process gave us a much broader view of the buyers and the buying process than the one held by the organization's staff up to this point. This new view then shaped the way the company would message each of these personas individually and also broadened the scope of the sales teams in their pursuit of these deals. In all, after developing the buyer insights, there were seven unique personas that were a part of the buying process. Not surprisingly, four of the seven personas that were identified had been routinely overlooked, and there was hardly any content that applied to all seven personas.

Knowing the key personas involved in the purchase process and having a clear understanding of the stages of the buying process is crucial to designing and delivering the relevant content that will stimulate the appropriate dialogue with buyers.

One Size Does Not Fit All

Understanding the buyers' role and involvement along the buying path is crucial and so is understanding their motivations and their view of the respective purchase. One size does not fit all in terms of demand generation content.

In the example of our software client, there were seven different personas involved and each had their own view on the purchase and their own motivations. As this was the case, content specific to those individual personas had to be developed to address their individual needs and concerns. Content created for the CFO could not be expected to appeal to an IT director and vice versa.

However, many organizations do not develop unique content for each persona aligned to each stage of the purchase process. Today, only 42.5 percent of companies consistently develop content that speaks to their buyers' pain points and challenges.[7] Moreover, the personas in the purchase process have their own unique view of pain points and challenges, and this increases the complexity.

For example, during a recent workshop on customized content development an attendee said, "We would never be able to do this; we have up to ten individual people involved in our buying process; we would literally be creating well over 100 new pieces of content." The task seemed overwhelming to him, but I was quick to explain that as buyers proceed through the unique initial purchase process, the view of the purchase and the individual needs and motivations start to move from an individual viewpoint to a corporate, more aligned view. This means that the Engage and early Nurture stages are the ones requiring the most individualized content, and as the buyers proceed to later stages and into the Conversion stage, they typically share a collective vision. However, an essential part of the content in the Engage stage is to address the individual's need while simultaneously looking to foster consensus among the various stakeholders. This is so vitally important because group conflict in the buying cycle is at its peak on average 37 percent of the way through the sales cycle.[8] Developing individual content that can at the same time promote consensus among all buyers is necessary.

Developing the Content Architecture

Too many organizations confuse a content calendar with their content architecture. At a B2B conference last year one of the attendees asked me to take a look at the content architecture his team had developed.

Figure 6.2 ANNUITAS Content Architecture Model.

Right away, I saw that the spreadsheet was aligned by month and showed a list of all the content assets the team wanted to deliver for that given month. This was not a content architecture, but simply an asset tracking spreadsheet and, at best, an editorial calendar. A content architecture (see figure 6.2) maps out the content that aligns to the Buyer Dialogue Logic and the corresponding purchase path.

A content architecture focuses on the conversation with buyers and answers the question of what content step comes next. This is different from a campaign or a one-and-done series of tactics that are so commonly used today and yield little in terms of pipeline, revenue, or buyer satisfaction. By mapping the Engage, Nurture, and Convert content to the buyers, marketers ensure continuity throughout the program from the buyers' perspective, which makes it easier for buyers to proceed through their purchase process and gain the education they want as they are being qualified for potential purchase.

Content First, Channel Second

Clients and prospects often ask me, "What tactics work best in B2B demand generation?" The real answer is, "It depends." Ultimately, the decision of what works and what does not work is up to the buyer and is part of the insights that need to be uncovered. Understanding buyers' content consumption patterns will provide the information needed to determine what kind of tactics will be most effective. The temptation to focus on the tactics—white paper, e-books, videos, and social media—rather than the substance of the content is very easy to succumb to. However, the most important part of content development is understanding the themes that will resonate with buyers. When developing content, organizations should consider the following questions:

- Does our content educate the buyers and speak to their pain points and challenges?
- Does our engage content focus too heavily on our product, services, and brand?
- Is our content written from the perspective of a subject matter expert or from our position as a vendor?

It is important to remember that although creating unique content by persona can seem overwhelming, variations on content can be delivered across multiple channels and through multiple tactics. A white paper can be partitioned out to deliver four or five blog posts and can then be condensed to be an e-book. Those blog posts can be used to feed the content of a monthly or quarterly newsletter. Marketers can use the same content, strategically, across a multitude of channels, each aligned to how buyers consume and interact with content. Keep in mind that there may be different content preferences across the various personas. What works for one buyer who has a role in the decision-making process will not necessarily work for another. Don't assume the IT director who consumes white papers regularly will spend hours on LinkedIn or Twitter to gain new information the way a vice president of marketing may do. Understanding these differences and planning for them will enhance the value and improve the interaction with content; rather than spending time creating content that is ineffective, organizations will most likely create less content, but generate more value from it.

A few years ago I had a conversation with Joe Chernov, former vice president of content for HubSpot about buyer-aligned content. In the discussion, Joe said something that marketers need to keep in mind: "We are not fighting for buyers' time, we are fighting for their attention." It was a brilliant insight and one that needs to be considered in every demand generation program. On average there are 121 business-related e-mails sent and received each day, and that number is expected to rise to 140 e-mails by 2018.[9] The amount of information being received and consumed is overwhelming. Buyers do not want to feel deluged during their buying process, and therefore developing content that captures their attention and is easy to access and consume will enhance the probability of the buyers interacting with it. According to the latest information from DemandGen Report, 91 percent of B2B buyers agree or strongly agree that they prefer "more interactive/visual content that they can access on demand."[10] This is the job of B2B demand generators, and organizations that do this effectively will see exponential improvement in their demand generation programs.

Qualifying Content

In addition to mapping the content architecture to the personas and their buying journey, content must also be aligned to the lead qualification model in order to provide the necessary insights into the buyers stage in their purchase process.

When implementing a demand generation program, many organizations develop content and then jump into lead scoring and begin assigning arbitrary numbers to content assets, for example, determining that white papers score ten points and e-books seven. What really matters, however, is where in the buyer's journey the buyer interacts with the content.

Referring to the buying process shown in figure 6.1, a buyer's interaction with ANNUITAS content at the beginning of the purchase process is not nearly as meaningful as the interaction with the content later, toward the end of the buying cycle. As content is built specifically to address either the Engage or Nurture stage, the interaction with content at various stages of the buyer's journey indicates intent and interest. Knowing this then eliminates the need to score content based on type. A white paper that is used in the Engage stage content according to the model may only receive 5 points, but a white paper that is used at the later stages of the Nurture stage may be get 25 points depending on the importance of the buyer participating in the dialogue.

In order to accurately track the interaction with the content offer (CO), the points assigned, and how they translate into where buyers are in their purchase journey the content should be coded. For instance, is the content more relevant in the Engage (E-CO) stage or in the Nurture stage (N-CO)? As the model above indicates, there will be many steps in the Engage and Nurture stages (depending on the buyers path to purchase), and having a code applied that corresponds to the qualification model and the buyers' place in the buying cycle will indicate the buyers' position on the path to purchase. This means that potentially, a buyer could have one interaction and be sent to sales as a highly qualified lead because the buyer's action indicates this person is well along in the purchase cycle and ready to be engaged on a personal rather than automated level. While this may be more the exception than the rule, allowing buyers to interact with the content as they want and qualifying these interactions by stage in the buying path versus type of content asset will provide more value to the content and generate a better qualified lead.

Optimizing Content

Demand generation is not all about the utilization of outbound channels but also includes the integration of inbound channels that will lead to better results. In an effort to drive these results, organizations must provide easy access to their content and make it easy to find. As buyers begin their purchase process, they are in the search of content that can help them frame their issues, and as noted earlier will most often search by using key phrases and terms. Having an understanding of these key search terms and phrases will help companies optimize their content, as each content asset should be searchable. This means that for every unique content asset that is part of an organization's demand generation program there should be one customized, optimized landing page buyers can access when conducting a search that leads them to the content. It is more effort to develop unique pages, but having one form for all content will limit your ability to drive inbound traffic and will not allow you to determine what stage of the purchase journey buyers have reached.

Relevant content is the key component in any successful demand generation program. However, it takes work to gain insights into buyers and to map these to their buying process. Currently, 70–80 percent of marketing content goes unused in B2B organizations[11] because most organizations do not have the information needed and are not taking the time to build effective, buyer-aligned content. Taking a defined and methodical approach to the development of content for demand generation will reduce the churn of unqualified leads and eliminate ineffective content, and it will increase the overall value and effectiveness of demand generation.

CHAPTER 7

Adapting the Lead Management Process

In a 2010 survey Frost & Sullivan asked B2B marketers what their top obstacles were in getting the most from their marketing automation systems; the top answer was "We do not have the right processes."[1] Fast-forward to 2015, and we find that many organizations are still struggling with changing their lead management process. As a result, they are also struggling to take advantage of increased demand generation budgets and marketing automation. Having a defined lead management process is the ingredient that binds together content strategy and organizational structure and allows better use of technology.

Lead management is defined as a process by which leads are qualified, scored, and managed throughout the buying process. This specific layer of the Demand Process necessitates that organizations have defined categories and a shared understanding between marketing and sales on what constitutes a qualified lead and on the process by which all leads will be handled. This ensures that no qualified leads are lost or left unattended. While this may seem like a simple task, it is often one of the most difficult areas of demand generation to define. This all too often leads to poor lead responsiveness, misalignment between marketing and sales teams, and, most important, a poor buying experience for prospects.

Several years ago I was working with an enterprise software firm that had told us they had established a defined lead management process, which was managed by the marketing automation and CRM technologies. During our work with company, we quickly uncovered that the process was not at all defined; the only approach the firm's marketers took to lead management was to pass leads on to the sales team as soon as a potential buyer had filled in a form in response to a marketing offer. Not surprisingly, the lead conversion rates were extremely low, which led to frustration in the sales force. In addition, because the company sold numerous products, many of which were purchased by the same individual, it was common for that one buyer to receive multiple phone calls from different sales reps who were all trying to sell their different products. Thus, not only was the sales team continually frustrated with the lack of "real leads," but the buyers were also growing frustrated with contacts from many sales reps. (one sales rep informed us that he was yelled at by a prospect who had informed him this was the fourth phone call he had received from the company and he was no longer inclined to want to do business with them due to being harassed).

I work with many organizations, and most of them struggle to define an optimal process that allows them to manage leads effectively. As a result, these companies are losing the ability to turn marketing from a cost center into a revenue engine. This is a huge loss of opportunity for many reasons; most important, Gartner states that companies that automate lead management processes can see an increase in revenue by at least 10 percent within six to nine months.[2]

In order to maximize their revenue potential, demand generation organizations need to develop a lead management process that includes the following:

- Lead routing definitions
- Lead qualification model
- Lead scoring model
- Progressive profile model
- Service level agreements

Automating Lead Management

While much of the lead management process can be automated via the integration of marketing automation and CRM systems, there still seems to be some confusion about what this means. Simply having automation and CRM technologies does not deliver lead management or define and end-to-end process. A 2014 survey of marketing leaders by Regalix highlights this confusion: 89 percent of marketers listed "Improved Lead Management and Lead Nurturing" as the number one benefit of their marketing automation system.[3] The study later indicates that 45 percent of respondents named lack of strategy as one of the largest roadblocks to marketing automation success. As lead management is fundamental to a demand process strategy, it would seem that many, just like companies in 2010, are still struggling to achieve success; they seem to be waiting for the technology to deliver success. The reality is that a lead management process will not be delivered via technology. The technology can only enable what has already been defined.

In addition to thinking that marketing automation can deliver lead management, B2B marketers lean too heavily on marketing automation in qualifying their leads. Several studies have shown that up to 70 percent of all leads generated by marketing are not followed up on by the sales teams. It seems reasonable then for marketers to think that to reverse this trend they should automate the qualification process and automatically route leads to sales. However, this approach has several flaws. First, many of these automated "leads" are sent on after the buyers' first interaction, at least in 21.7 percent of organizations that still follow this approach. Automating the process can increase efficiency, but when inquiries are routed to sales as leads, this will only increase the percentage of leads that are ignored. Second, the problem with using only automation in the qualification of leads is the lack of human interaction. No matter how good a lead qualification process is or how rigorous the lead scoring model is, having no human interaction and only passing automated leads to sales teams is a flawed practice. Even though in most cases today's buying process is largely digital, there is still a need for a human interaction during the qualification process, as the B2B buying process still involves people. Having human interaction as part of the lead qualification process allows organizations and buyers to ask each other questions, develop deeper insights, and make a human connection that can serve to further endear the organization and brand to them. However, only 41.5 percent of organizations use this approach when qualifying their leads.[4]

I have seen many organizations employ an inside sales or telemarketing approach to help qualify opportunities as part of their demand generation programs, and this can be a very effective practice if done correctly. However, a good number of these calls are inserted far too early in the buying cycle. For example, I have worked with one company that has a practice of calling people after their first download of a marketing asset. I decided to test how this approach worked so I downloaded a content asset and was called nine times within a two-week period in an attempt to be qualified for sales. This approach, which is used by many organizations, of calling individuals immediately upon a download of an asset is missing any real opportunity for qualification because the likelihood of a buyer being ready to purchase after one interaction is very low. After all, the average B2B buyer consumes three to five pieces of content before engaging with a sales person.[5] This function of qualification by telephone should be placed at a later stage of the lead nurturing process. Once these leads are deemed qualified by the telemarketing function, they can then be passed along to field sales teams for further engagement. Leads that do not meet the qualification standards will be sent back to the nurture stage of the demand generation program until buyers indicate by their interactions with the program that they are ready for another follow-up call from the lead qualification team.

Defining the Stages of the Lead Management Process

In a meeting with a client, a leading vendor in the help desk market, we outlined the company's current lead management process on a whiteboard, listing the first step as inquiry. By the company's definition, an inquiry occurred every time an individual filled out a web form. When I asked the client what the next step in the process was, one of the marketing directors said, "We take that inquiry and automatically route it to sales for follow-up." Before I could begin writing that on the board, one of the other directors said, "That's not entirely accurate." She explained that new inquiries are first sent to the telemarketing team for qualification. If the prospects are not reached after seven attempts, the inquiry goes back into the database. As the meeting showed, many of the individuals had a different understanding of the process the company used to manage and convert leads.

This situation is not uncommon, and it shows that B2B demand generation organizations need to take the time necessary to define the steps of their lead management process. To do this both marketing and sales personnel (including marketing and sales ops) must work together to define how they manage leads, from the initial filling out of a form on the web all the way to closing of the sale. Taking this approach will show where potential gaps exist in the current process. Second, this approach will bring consensus to the group on the best process to align to the buyers' purchase path. I led a lead management session of this kind for a client and the head of sales operations stated, "I knew we had some disjointed steps in our process, but seeing it all laid out brings some reality to the problem." Having the details of the lead management defined and agreed to by both marketing and sales teams will bring clarity to the process and ensure all qualified leads get the proper follow-up so that the organization can capitalize on the most qualified leads.

In organizations where I have seen the process defined, it is usually defined up to the point when the qualified lead gets passed on to the sales team. However, there are still steps that need to be defined beyond the sales qualified lead (SQL) stage. As part of the lead routing definition, organizations should include the sales opportunity stages as well, and these typically include several discrete phases. In addition, the lead routing needs to include a "turn back" option that sales can use to pass back leads that are not ready to buy once a discussion with the prospect has been established or the prospect is not able to be reached. The lead then goes back into the demand generation program for further nurturing. This routing path is essential because it ensures that buyers will be continually engaged in dialogue while their behavior is tracked. At the right time, the lead is then promoted again to qualified lead status and again turned over to the sales team. Without this option of turning back the lead potential buyers stay in the CRM system and receive no further nurturing during a potentially active buying process, and this puts any potential deal at risk.

What Is a Lead? The Importance of
a Lead Qualification Model

Ask ten marketing and ten sales people what the definition of a lead is and most likely you will end up with twenty different answers. Yet, nearly 40 percent of B2B organizations still do not have a common definition of a lead that is shared by marketing and sales teams.[6] This leaves end-to-end demand generation to guesswork and is one of the reasons why many marketing departments are failing to meet the needs of their sales teams in delivering qualified leads. If there is no common understanding on what is needed, the ability to meet that goal will be iffy at best.

For a robust approach to lead management it is essential to have a definition of your lead qualification model, which goes beyond defining what a lead is. Organizations must define each and every stage of their lead qualification model starting with the definition of an inquiry all the way to a closed-won or closed-lost deal. While this may seem fairly straightforward (which is one of the reasons why many marketing departments attempt to assign these definitions on their own), it is not. There are many steps to be considered in a qualification model. Over 70 percent of B2B enterprise demand generation organizations measure inquiries, marketing qualified leads (MQLs), SQLs, and closed won deals.[7] However, such a broad qualification model does not properly align to the Engage, Nurture, and Conversion steps buyers take when seeking to make a purchase. In my work with clients, most of the buyers we interview go through multiple steps and interactions from the time of their first inquiry until they reach a point of being truly marketing qualified. Adding more granularity to the lead qualification model with definitions of each stage will better align the qualification model to the buying process. An effective lead qualification model identifies the stages B2B buyers are going through from the beginning to the end of their purchase process. That is, having stages such as pre-MQL or qualified engaged (which would be between the inquiry and the MQL stage) will better qualify all the leads throughout the buying process and enable the demand generation team to better forecast the lead pipeline. Similarly, qualified leads should be designated qualified warm leads or qualified hot leads so sales reps can better identify leads that should receive priority in follow-up.

Building up the lead qualification process and model is a fundamental step in identifying the buyers' purchase path and is the foundation of a robust scoring model. The more precise demand generation marketers can be in aligning the lead qualification model to the buyers' journey (content model and buyer dialogue logic), the better they can ensure that only the highest qualified leads will be passed on to the sales teams.

Lead Scoring

B2B organizations face four fundamental problems when it comes to developing a lead scoring model. The first issue is that many organizations are jumping to scoring leads before defining their qualification approach simply because scoring can easily be done with marketing automation. A few years ago a prospect from a large B2B enterprise in the marketing services and technology sector and I discussed the company's approach to demand generation. The senior vice president described the current state of affairs, the challenges, and the successes. When I asked what role he envisioned for us in helping, he said, "What we really need is a robust lead scoring model so we can get more from our marketing automation." In reality this was the last thing the company needed at that point. This organization had limited insight into buyers: how they purchase, who is involved with the purchase, or how they consume content; all this is critical information that needs to be scored. I tried to persuade that senior vice president that building a lead scoring model should be part of the overall process, but to do it now would be premature and simply doing this for the sake of automation. Simply trying to build a scoring model based on the capabilities of marketing automation will not provide the benefits looked for and may do more harm by producing false positives in the lead scoring. This in turn will cast a bad light on the entire demand generation strategy, and this is what gets marketing and sales departments arguing over the misperception of the leads generated.

The second challenge many organizations face is using an outdated approach to their lead scoring. For example, early in my career I worked for a B2B marketing agency that had an outbound call center focused on generating leads for our clients. Most of the calling was in response to our clients marketing campaigns; other calls were cold calls to contacts from a database of names the client provided. Leads were scored and qualified based on the prospects' budget, authority, need, and timeframe (BANT) to purchase. Depending on the answers of the prospects, they were assigned a lead score rating of A (being the most qualified) through D. This type of lead qualification was commonplace for most of our clients and their programs; back then, buyers had limited ability to get information, and the sales representatives controlled most of the buying process. As the buying process has fundamentally changed over the past 15–20 years, this model no longer should be the scoring approach organizations take. Yet, I still encounter companies relying on this antiquated approach for scoring leads, and some go as so far to use the BANT questions on their web forms. While the BANT questions can be useful when speaking to a prospect one-on-one, they should not be used to score leads that will then be deemed qualified and sent to the lead qualification or sales teams for follow-up.

According to several studies, including those conducted by MarketingSherpa and JanRain, more than 50 percent of B2B buyers will lie on web forms when asked for custom information (beyond general contact data). This means it is more of a challenge to have truly qualified leads to be sent to sales teams; after all, more than half of the BANT data collected could be false.

The third issue most common in lead scoring is that many models are purely one- dimensional in nature and score either by demographic or by behavior, but not necessarily both. In fact, when asked how they score leads, 48.1 percent of B2B demand generation marketers stated they score on behavioral elements, and only 34.9 percent stated that they score on demographic details, such as title and the seniority level of the individual. Fewer than 30 percent of marketers score on account demographics, such as industry and revenue size. Let's use ANNUITAS as an example: we focus our services on B2B enterprises with revenues in excess of $1 billion. We have specific personas that we target in those accounts, and we know the demographics of our customers. There are many individuals who come to our website, consume our content, and respond to our offers. However, if we focused only on these behavioral aspects of these "leads," we would have a serious problem when selling because all the individuals who are outside our ideal buyer demographic would also be viewed as qualified leads based on their behavior. To get a full picture of lead quality and ensure the leads fit the ideal buyer profile, companies need scoring that is multidimensional.

Two other factors that contribute to poor outcomes of lead scoring models are the scoring of assets rather than of position and the lack of an active interest threshold (AIT). First, as explained previously, many organizations design their scoring models by assigning a score to the specific asset that is accessed by their prospects. Generally speaking, white papers or webinar attendance receives the highest scores, and e-books and webinar registrations receive lower scores. However, the scoring should have a higher importance and value based on where in the buyers' journey an action is being taken, rather than depend entirely on the type of asset consumed. If a buyer has been an active participant in the program and moved through the Engage stage and is now interacting with content that has been designed for the later Nurture stages, this content of the later Nurture stage should be scored higher because it indicates the buyer's position on the purchase path. The buyer at this point is closer to interacting with the sales team, is more highly qualified, and indicates intent. Simply scoring based on asset type does not provide this type of indication and may merely indicate a content preference. Second, including AIT as a component of the scoring model means that organizations will be able to potentially "hold back" buyers who may have stopped their participation in the program. The AIT defines a minimal level of interaction buyers must maintain in order to keep their active status in the program and not be moved to a nurture drip track. By adding regression factors into the model, such as lapses in activity, it is possible to reduce the overall AIT and "pull the buyer back" from being scored further and thus moving to the next qualification stage unless new activity resumes.

A final consideration regarding lead scoring is the use of "accelerators." These are rules that should be built into the scoring model; these rules automatically qualify a lead as "qualified hot" due to the action taken by the buyer. For example, one of the clients we have worked with is a large enterprise industrial manufacturing company, as part of the firm's demand generation approach, marketers wanted to have buyers test their product. Rather than make buyers walk through a series of content steps to get to that point, buyers can request a test of the product at any time. When a buyer makes this request, the person is automatically scored as a hot qualified lead and routed to the sales team as this is a strong buying signal and should be addressed immediately. Organizations developing their lead scoring model should think about the areas that may be an accelerator for their buyers, such as a request for a demo, a request for a quote, or a request to speak to the sales department. While there will not be many of these accelerators, there will be some that signal a high propensity to buy, and responding accordingly will increase the likelihood of closing the deal.

Lead scoring is an important component of any strategic demand generation program but cannot be developed in isolation. It is a step in the lead management process, not a process unto itself.

Taking a Progressive Profiling Approach

The belief that it is necessary to capture as much information about a prospect in the first interaction as possible is limiting the success of many demand generation departments. For example, I worked with one of the largest software companies in the world and found that the firm's web forms have ten required fields a prospect had to fill out before being able to access the desired asset. If a prospect is going to go to that length to acquire the asset, then, as noted previously, much of the information entered into the form will be false. However, the more likely scenario is that the prospect will abandon the form and not participate in any way. The average conversion rate for lead generation forms stands at 11 percent.[8] While several reasons contribute to this low rate—some which have been discussed above, such as lack of compelling content or content that is not focused on the buyer—undoubtedly, one of the biggest causes is the number of fields required to gain access to a specific asset. This underscores the importance of having a progressive profiling process to collect information. Progressive profiling is the practice of collecting information on buyers gradually. Considering that most buyers begin their purchase journey through a digital medium, the only two pieces of information needed to begin that dialogue with buyers is their name and e-mail address. This puts a low barrier of access in front of buyers and increases the chances that they will supply this information. As a demand genera-tion program should be designed to be perpetual in nature, the follow-up might be an offer to that buyer of a second piece of content that would then require additional information. Perhaps then the form could ask for the company name and revenue size and so on. Over time, not only will a full profile on the prospective buyer be obtained, but rapport with the buyer and the buyer's trust are also developed.

Marketo ran a study a number of years ago on the impact of progressive profiling and having fewer fields on web forms. The study tested separate forms of nine, seven, and five fields. The results showed that reducing the number of form fields from nine to five increased the overall conversion rates of those fields by 34 percent. The study also revealed that the shorter five- field form reduced the overall cost of conversion by \$10.66 per lead.[9] Considering the impact that this can have on a demand generation pro-gram these are significant numbers that will increase the number of quali-fied leads as well as drive a higher overall ROI.

To Gate or Not To Gate?

I have been asked many times "When should we gate our content or what assets should we gate versus giving them away?" When it comes to driv-ing demand, all the assets that are part of a demand generation program should be gated as the entire purpose behind a strategic program is to begin a dialogue with prospects and convert them into buyers.

Service Level Agreements

The best designed lead management process can quickly unravel if there is no assurance that sales representatives are following up on the quali-fied leads that are generated by marketing. A 2013 study conducted by the American Marketing Association showed that 70 percent of mar-keting leads go unattended by sales reps.[10] This practice is detrimental to any demand generation success and is one of the key reasons why marketing and sales departments need to have established SLAs to manage and govern the approach they will take to the handling of the lead. Currently, less than 38 percent of B2B enterprise organizations have SLAs in place,[11] but these agreements can make or break the success of a program.

SLAs need to align to the lead qualification model and govern the stages when leads become qualified and are sent on to the sales team. The SLA should also define the team responsible (marketing or sales), the action that needs to be taken, and the time frame in which that action needs to occur. For instance, when a lead is qualified as a "hot lead" and accepted by sales, the action could be as follows:

Lead development team (LDT) inspects the leads and checks for data quality and conducts a follow-up both by e-mail and phone. If the criteria is met (according to the lead qualification model), the LDT gets sales reps' agreement on the viability and acceptance of the lead and creates the opportunity in the CRM system. The dispensation time frame in responding to that hot qualified lead would be four hours while the conversion time frame from qualified to accepted could be anywhere from one to four days.

Having these rules developed and agreed to by marketing and sales departments ensures that there is a system of checks and balances and protects the investment that is being made in demand generation. At the same time, these rules ensure that the buyers are getting a timely response when they are ready to move onto the Conversion stage.

The administration of the SLAs can be something that is automated in the CRM technology with lead alerts, reminders, and the use of dashboards that can show the response time of reps on leads. Marketing leaders in one company I spoke with not long ago understood the importance of fast response times from their reps, and they enforced the SLAs by sending leads that had passed the time frame in a sales rep's queue to another rep. This had a significant impact on the results and altered the behavior of their team dramatically.

Adopting and implementing a lead management process is key to ensuring demand generation transformation in any organization. The need to qualify, score, and manage leads effectively and efficiently cannot be overstated; yet, this is an area where marketing continues to struggle and where 68 percent of B2B organizations still do not have a defined "sales funnel."[12] Investing the time, money, and resources to develop lead management will improve demand generation dramatically and speed up transformation.

CHAPTER 8

Measuring for Success

One of the areas that vex B2B marketers the most is that of metrics and analytics. For example, the head of demand generation for a large manufacturing company told me the biggest struggle his teams currently face is "proving the value of their demand generation activities." And he is not alone. In a study conducted by the ITSMA and VisionEdge Marketing, only 26 percent of B2B organizations reported to be "able to measure and report on the contributions of the program to the business."[1]

Despite all the discussions about the rise and importance of big data in B2B, the reality is that much of this data lacks the necessary context, and therefore marketers are not generating the necessary insights they need to optimize their demand generation programs and investments. According to the CMO survey conducted by Duke University's Fuqua School of Business, 6.4 percent of marketing budgets are allocated to marketing analytics, and that figure is expected to double in the next three years. However, less than one-third of marketing projects use marketing analytics, and only 30.4 percent of organizations formally evaluate the value of their marketing analytics.[2]

The other challenge CMOs and marketing leaders must address when it comes to demand generation measurement and analysis is that most of their personnel do not have the skills or knowledge to properly measure marketing performance and marketing ROI—with or without increased budgets for analytics. According to the Fournaise Marketing Group, "90 percent of marketers are not trained in Marketing Performance and Marketing ROI."[3]

If B2B marketers are to be successful in modernizing their programs and driving overall transformation, they have to address the challenges of measurement and analytics in two ways. The first is establishing a set of metrics that makes both the individual program's and the overall demand generation's performance visible. There are very few organizations that have established the right KPIs to make this possible, and furthermore, many do not have the right technology solutions to go to the depths of analysis that is needed. Second, marketers need to address the current skills and knowledge gap because trying to demonstrate ROI without knowing the financial impact will not meet the needs of today's businesses.

Measuring the Right Outcomes

Demand generation is an outcome-oriented discipline. However, many demand generation professionals struggle to measure the outcomes and instead are measuring their activity—the number of clicks, visits to the website, impressions, etc. For example, I know of one large enterprise organization in the financial services sector that has "number of names added to the marketing database" as one of its top KPIs. With this as one of the top goals, the company is succeeding because it has well over 30 million names in its database. However, there is no value to this metric in terms of successful demand generation because the firm's marketers cannot make a connection between the growth of their database and the program's ROI. This is an example of measuring the activity but failing to tie the results to any meaningful business outcome.

The KPIs that matter include the by-product or outcomes of the activity or program. How many qualified leads came from the programs? How many of the qualified leads converted to pipeline and ultimately to revenue? What are the conversion rates at the various stages of the buying funnel? Having insight into these metrics allows organizations to continually fine-tune their approach and maximize their conversion rates while optimizing the outcomes. These are the metrics that matter to the business, and it is expected that those who manage demand generation for their organizations can clearly report the value these measurements provide.

Unfortunately, among large enterprise B2B organizations two of the most frequently tracked demand generation metrics are website traffic at 71.7 percent and impressions at 51.9 percent.[4] While these metrics can be leading indicators of buyers' initial interest, they are not the kind of business outcome metrics that will be of interest to CEOs because they do not provide any true value or show how demand generation is maximizing CLV. CEOs and CFOs want to know the critical financial metrics that drive the business; they want to have a clear picture of how marketing investments are affecting pipeline and revenue. Certain metrics are important to have from a marketing perspective, but these alone do not demonstrate the function's contribution to business growth or provide the insights necessary to inform sound business decisions.

Starting With the End in Mind

Organizations often struggle with performance measurement because there is no set goal of the outcomes their programs are to achieve before they initiate them. General goals such as "drive more leads to sales" or "increase lead quality" are too vague and make it hard, if not impossible, to measure and analyze for any meaningful insight. As part of the development of any demand generation program, clear conversion, pipeline, and revenue goals with hard numbers assigned to them need to be stated. Furthermore, a quantitative analysis needs to be conducted to properly forecast the results of the program and provide a goal for the marketing teams against which to measure their performance. Conducting this kind of detailed analysis can be quite complex, however, and if this is new to the organization, it is advisable to start simply by applying some "reverse funnel math." To build this type of model, organizations will, at a minimum, need to know the following information:

- What is the overall corporate revenue objective for the line of business for which marketers will be generating demand?
- What is marketing's expected contribution to the overall revenue goal?

- What is the average sales price of the products, solutions, or services for that line of business?
- What are the current funnel conversion metrics?
- What is the average sales price?

Additional information that will be helpful but not essential is:

- What is the total addressable target market for the product or service?
- What is the average sales cycle for the product or service?
- What is the current count of the database that is part of the addressable market?

One of the difficulties I often see in demand generation is that much of the basic information listed above is unknown in many organizations. For example, a colleague of mine was working with the vice president of marketing of an organization that specialized in the health care industry to establish a high-level business case for investing in demand generation. The client wanted to present this business case to his executive team in an attempt to get additional funding. He could not answer questions about average sales cycle and funnel conversion rates, and was not sure where to find this information. By working backward from the total revenue number, marketers will be able to determine and measure basic ROI goals; this is something currently only 21 percent of organizations are able to do.[5]

Managing and Measuring the Buyers' Journey

While measuring the basic ROI of demand generation programs is important and serves as a proof of success, on its own it will not provide the kind of insight needed to continually optimize and consistently report on a demand generation program. Given that demand generation is a perpetual, program-based activity, it requires analytics and business intelligence to be applied continuously so the process and content can be fine-tuned over time and produce the greatest yield. To accomplish this, as with all other areas of demand generation, it is essential to understand the buyers and their path to purchase. While many companies are looking to align their content in this manner, very few are structuring their KPIs to align to the buying process; this is one of the reasons why organizations struggle to measure their demand generation outcomes. Currently, only 17.9 percent of organizations have demand generation performance KPIs for each stage of the buying process that measure both the online and offline buyer behavior.[6]

Like content that is aligned to Engage, Nurture, Convert cadences, the KPIs that need to be tracked and measured also need to map to these three steps. This approach is radically different from what is commonly done in most organizations that only look to measure campaign (one-and-done) performance. However, measuring at a more granular level like this will provide the business intelligence needed to continually optimize the program and derive greater value from it over time. Only then will marketers clearly see buyers' unique content consumption patterns throughout the entire buying journey.

Core Demand Generation KPIs

While demonstrating ROI and revenue results of demand generation programs is the ultimate goal, having a clear understanding of how this was achieved is imperative. In order to accomplish this, organizations need to change their approach as well as what they are measuring in order to demonstrate demand generation performance. There are six core KPIs that demand generation departments need to implement in order to measure their performance at the level of both the individual program and the total demand process. These core KPIs are as follows:

- engagement performance
- content performance
- nurturing e-mail performance
- lead management performance
- revenue performance
- return on investment performance

These six categories will provide the necessary insight into the discrete phases of the demand generation program and will at the same time, when viewed in total, allow for the measurement and reporting on the program as a whole.

Engagement Performance

The measurement of the Engage stage focuses on channel performance and the costs of that channel or medium. With insights into the channel performance, organizations will be able to make better decisions on the channels they should invest in to attract more prospects into their demand generation programs. More specifically, the engagement performance KPIs measure the following:

- Number of Prospect Impressions by Channel—this number measures the various touchpoints with potential prospects whether or not the prospect chose to download the content offer (asset). This analysis is conducted by individual channel as it will provide insight into the best performing medium for buyers.
- Number of "Engaged" by Channel—this measurement is aligned to the lead qualification model and measures the channel that has the largest contribution to the engaged stage of the lead qualification model. Again, this is important to understand as pay-per-click (PPC) may have a better performance for driving potential buyers into the program compared to social media or outbound e-mail via a targeted list rental. Having this insight will guide future investments and also provide further insight into the buyers' content consumption preferences.
- Prospect to Engaged Conversion Ratio by Channel—this measurement is also aligned to the lead qualification model and measures the conversion from an impression to the engaged state. This is also measured by the individual channels as it cannot be assumed that just because one channel is driving impressions it will be an optimal channel for converting those impressions into engaged stage leads.
- Total Engagement Cost by Channel—many marketers seek to measure the cost per lead as part of their overall demand generation performance tracking. However, measuring the cost per channel is

equally important especially when compared to the average size of a deal. Analyzing this metric allows organizations to determine the value of that channel and eventually use this information to determine a true ROI.

- Cost per Impression and per Engaged by Channel—these measurements, much like the Total Engagement Cost by Channel, are the beginning points of being able to hone in on an ROI and quantitative analysis of the demand generation program. These two metrics show the average cost per impression by the various engagement channels and also what it is costing the organization to deliver an "Engaged" stage buyer into the program by individual channel. Understanding this allows further insight into what is the most cost-effective channel to drive both impressions and engaged leads.

- Cost per Revenue by Channel—this is measuring what costs the organization incurs for every $1 spent by engagement channel. Understanding what the organization is paying to achieve revenue is a must, and having this information at every stage of the buying cycle (by aligning it to the lead qualification model) will provide the needed insight to properly calculate ROI and justify the spending on various media.

Content Performance

The fuel for any demand generation program is content. B2B marketers need to stop simply creating more content and instead shift their focus to creating relevant, buyer-centric content. The only way this will be accomplished is when demand generation teams begin to analyze the performance of their program content. If these metrics are not tracked, B2B marketers will be flying blind, not knowing what areas to optimize and what content is resonating with their prospective buyers and customers. The content performance KPIs measure the following:

- The submit rate by content offer—This measures the conversion rate from initial impression to download by the individual content offer.
- Content offer downloads—This is simply knowing how many downloads have occurred of the individual content offer.

- Lead stage elasticity by content offer—This measurement is aligned to the lead qualification model and measures the propensity of the content offer to yield a buyer at a given qualification stage.
- Lead stage velocity by content offer—This measures the average time between the download of the content offer and the buyer reaching a given lead qualification stage. This measurement provides insight that marketers can use to increase the velocity at which leads progress through the buying process. If through demand generation programs marketers can increase lead and deal velocity by even ten days, what will that mean in terms of revenue for the business? This is something marketers need to be able to show as further proof of their impact on pipeline and revenue.
- Content offer cost—This is measuring the production cost of each content offer.
- Attributed revenue by content offer—This measures the total revenue attributed to the download of the content offer.
- Cost per attributed revenue by content offer—This measures the average cost per $1 of revenue by each content offer.

Nurturing E-mail Performance

Nurturing is the link between the Engagement and Conversion stages and is most often the area of demand generation programs that is automated. Given the nature of automation in this stage, the e-mail performance of the Nurture stage must be measured and analyzed. This is not to indicate that e-mail should not be analyzed at the Engage or Convert stages as well, but the Nurture stage requires greater use of e-mail, hence the focus is justified.

Many B2B organizations already track and measure e-mail performance. Given their use of marketing automation, however, measuring this in isolation only provides a small window into the overall program performance and does not allow for optimization of the overall program. The nurturing e-mail performance KPIs measure the following:

- Number of e-mails sent—This is measuring the number of unique outbound e-mails sent.

- Open rate by Nurture e-mail—This measures the open rate (versus the number sent) per unique nurture e-mail.
- Click rate—This measures the number of unique clicks (versus the number sent) per unique Nurturing e-mail.
- Hard bounce rate per Nurture e-mail—This refers to the number of hard bounces that occur for each Nurture e-mail. Keep in mind that an overly high number of hard bounces indicates data integrity issues and indicates the need for more investment in data hygiene.
- Soft bounce rate per Nurture e-mail—This refers to the number of soft bounces per unique Nurture -mail.

Lead Management Performance

Most of the B2B marketing teams I speak to have adopted some version of their own "sales funnel" or "lead waterfall" as a way to track their conversion rates from initial prospect engagement to close. However, additional KPIs need to be applied because simply measuring the conversion rate only gives a partial view of how buyers are progressing from one stage to the next. The more information and data marketers can use to enhance the programs, the more they will be able to improve and optimize these programs and the better the outcomes. The lead management performance KPIs measure the following:

- Number of buyers by individual lead stage—This information will provide marketing teams with the insight necessary to better set and achieve their revenue contribution goals.
- Conversion rates by lead stage—This is what most marketing organizations do in some form or another. However, there are often gaps in this process as the stages measured may be far too broad. In order to get more refined results, demand generation teams should build more granular steps into their conversion funnels. Most conversion models measure inquiry (a contact who fills out a form) as the first stage and then MQL as their second stage. Given that there is often a good amount of buyer activity from buyer's first contact or inquiry to the MQL stage, B2B demand generation teams would improve their

conversion models by building in additional stages and measuring that activity accordingly.

- Velocity by lead stage—This measures the average time it takes prospects to move from one lead stage to the next. This KPI is very important because it identifies potential lags that may occur between one stage and the next, and this KPI will provide some clarity about the potential cause of the delays. Marketers can then remedy any issues and optimize the program to ensure a continuous progression through the program.

- Growth rate by lead stage—This measures the percentage increase in the number of buyers at each lead qualification stage. Over time, the aggregate number of buyers at each stage should continue to increase. Having a disproportionate number of leads stuck in one stage would indicate an issue with the program either at the content conversion level or with the sales responsiveness in accepting and further engaging the leads in conversation.

- Key conversion arcs—This measures the conversion rates between key lead qualification stages. Sirius Decisions, Forrester, and CEB have all published data on industry best-in-class conversion rates. Knowing the number of engaged leads that are converting to hot qualified leads and then to close represents baseline intelligence necessary to consistently improve the performance along these key stages.

- Nurture database size—This measures the total number of "nurturable" contacts that have opted in. This tells marketers how many active dialogues they are having as a result of their program and thus indicates the relevance of their content for buyers.

Revenue Performance

The measurement of demand generation revenue performance enables CMOs and B2B marketers to speak about the business impact of their programs. The revenue performance KPIs measure the following:

- Pipeline value by lead stage—This measures the estimated pipeline value by each lead qualification stage. Knowing this information and the conversion metrics allows demand generation teams to forecast the pipeline and revenue that will be realized from their programs.

- Closed revenue value by demand generation program—This measures the total closed revenue by demand generation program.
- Pipeline growth rate by lead stage—This measures the rate of growth in the pipeline over time by individual lead stage. As the program progresses, the pipeline by stage should increase as more potential buyers will be coming into the program.
- Closed revenue growth rate by program—This measures the cumulative growth in revenue by individual demand generation program.
- Win rate by demand generation program—This measures the number of closed wins the sales team achieves as a result of qualified leads delivered by each individual program.

The revenue performance metrics applied to each individual program should also be rolled up to show the overall performance of the demand generation operation and the impact is has on revenue generation for the business.

Return on Investment Performance KPIs

In order to truly measure to business outcomes, demand generation needs to have a positive net present value (NPV). When analyzing programs that get to a positive ROI, organizations need to take this into account. Measuring NPV compares the negative and positive cash flows over a certain time period to determine the total return on the demand generation investment. I have rarely seen a marketing organization conduct this kind of analysis, but marketers who want to be seen as revenue generators for their organizations need to begin measuring to this level of detail and must view demand generation through a financial lens.

Managing Marketing as a Business

Many people in B2B marketing and demand generation professionals tell me that they are viewed as a cost center to their organization. This view of marketing by corporate leaders is keeping CMOs from having a seat at the executive table. This perception is due to marketers not applying an analytical lens to their demand generation practices, not using financial terms to communicate results, and not justifying the investments made in marketing as driving revenue. When marketing departments are viewed as a cost center, they are often the first to have their budget cut when organizations seek cost savings as a way to increase their margin. However, when demand generation is managed as a business, including analysis of revenue, ROI, and NPV, this empowers CMOs to manage marketing as a business and report on their own profit and loss (P&L) just like other lines of business in an organization. However, most demand generation departments are not applying a critical, analytical lens to their activities, and less than 45 percent of them measure their contribution to revenue, and 0 percent measure their contribution to pipeline.[7] In order for marketing teams to make the needed transformation, they must apply business intelligence to their craft. The canned, basic reports that come from marketing automation and CRM systems today will not provide the critical insights necessary.

Currently, only 32.1 percent of enterprise B2B marketing organizations use business intelligence as part of their technology stack.[8] The ownership and understanding of business intelligence is another shift that B2B marketers need to make in their quest to advance and modernize demand generation. Without the deeper analysis and insight this technology allows, marketing departments can optimize demand generation only manually and incrementally. As part of their growing technology bundle, B2B marketing departments must consider acquiring a BI tool that will enable them to do the sophisticated analysis needed to properly report, analyze, and optimize their programs.

Closing the Skills Gap in Marketing Measurement

As highlighted earlier in this chapter, there is a tremendous knowledge gap in today's marketing organizations regarding their ability to measure marketing performance at the business level. The adoption and analysis of new KPIs that demonstrate revenue outcomes is not something B2B marketers have had to do in the past, so it is not reasonable to expect that those who have never been trained to do this kind of analysis will acquire these skills on the job. As part of the growth and development of the demand generation practice in marketing, CMOs should look to create a position(s) of data analyst as part of their organization. An individual with these skills may already work for the organization, but if not, the budget should be adjusted to allow bringing staff with these skills into the organization. For example, I know one large electronics manufacturing organization that recently hired a PhD in analytics just for this purpose. In her role she works with the demand generation team members to forecast the quantitative outcomes of their programs, and she also runs their business intelligence to analyze and optimize the programs over time. This role, while not typically found in the demand generation organization, will become more commonplace in the future. Staffing this role is one of the hiring changes CMOs need to consider so their organizations can become more scientific regarding generating demand.

Another option for bringing these skills to the marketing department is to work with the CFO whose department usually has staff with these analytical skills. Measurement of marketing performance is a continuous struggle that has troubled B2B marketing professionals for some time, as a 2006 article by Forrester Research shows[9]. However, there are no longer any excuses, and the issue must be addressed and resolved. Measuring the right KPIs (with context), acquiring the right technology to enable this insight, and acquiring the right skills and knowledge to bring the business intelligence to life are three major transformative steps CMOs must take to drive advancements in the demand process.

CHAPTER 9

Optimizing Data and Technology

Optimizing data and technology to best support demand generation programs is a must; yet, many organizations are limiting the success of their programs due to a lack of data, inadequate technology governance, and insufficient optimization.

The importance of having clean data to fuel demand generation programs cannot be overstated, but a vast number of companies neglect the integrity of their data. A study conducted by NetProspex on the health of marketing databases found the following:

- 84 percent of marketing databases are barely functional.
- 88 percent of marketing databases are lacking basic firmographic information, such as industry, verticals, and company revenue.
- 64 percent of database records do not contain a phone number.[1]

The chances of success with demand generation will be severely limited unless B2B organizations begin to apply stringent governance to the integrity and management of their data. In virtually every organization I have worked with there have been challenges surrounding the integrity of the database, including duplicates, bad e-mail addresses, partial records, and so on. In most of these firms, the marketing personnel generally are aware of that their data set is flawed; yet, little is done to address it. In fact, in 86 percent of organizations people think their data may be inaccurate in some way.[2] While the upkeep of marketing data is not the most glamorous of jobs in an organization, it is one of the most vital to ensure positive outcomes for demand generation.

Data Governance

One of the reasons many B2B organizations struggle so much with their data is there has been no defined governance for the management of it and a lack of alignment of the systems that house data to people, processes, and content.

Often, data is stored in different systems throughout the organization without a uniform process for entering data. In addition, often no rules are defined on who can access or manage the data, and this can quickly lead to data integrity issues. For example, I spoke with a client to review some of the reports we had run on the firm's marketing automation database, and the Senior Director of the Demand Center stated, "We will be able to control the data structure and governance coming from my organization, but we have no ability to control what is coming in from the other groups that also have access to our marketing automation and CRM systems." This is why data governance has to be a company-wide initiative: it has an impact on demand generation and will have a negative impact the overall performance of demand generation programs.

Recently, in a marketing meeting with one of the larger information services companies in the world, we worked with them in assessing the company's demand process and recommended the changes needed to improve the overall maturity of the demand process. As we discussed the company's difficulties with the management of its data and its approach to data governance, it soon became apparent that there was no data governance and no strategic approach to data use. The company had several marketing automation systems and two CRM systems. Not surprisingly, the company also had no standards for uploading data across the varied systems; as a result, there were numerous duplicates, incomplete records, and bad information, and the organization's ability to execute its demand generation programs effectively was impaired. At the end of our meeting the marketing operations manager said, "We just hope that none of our customers call in and ask what products they own, because we would never be able to tell them." This mismanagement of data was preventing the organization from effectively cross-selling to their customer base, which would have had a significant upside in terms of revenue. Although this is shocking to hear, it is not a surprise; as the NetProspex study pointed out, most organizations are in the same state.

There are some minimal governance standards that organizations can define and quickly implement to move toward data integrity; once these basics are established, organizations will then be able to add more standards and become more sophisticated over time. Some of the relevant considerations are as follows:

- Companies must determine who has access to the data and what level of control personnel has to add or delete records. For example, one organization had an "open data" policy. This meant that everyone in the company had full administrative rights to the sales and marketing data. This is obviously not a recommended approach. The fewer people have full administrative access to data, the less likely the chance of error. Simply defining the levels of access and permissions—full administrator as opposed to read-only access, and so on—will be a step forward in protecting data from corruption.

- Companies must identify what systems (marketing, finance, ERP, etc.) house the data and what systems must be integrated in order to get a full view of customers; what systems will be able to overwrite data in other systems must also be defined. Many enterprise organizations, like the one in the example above, have several marketing automation systems. In fact, of companies that are using a cloud-based automation system (as the majority are), as many as 50 percent are using more than one system,[3] and this only adds to the complexity and difficulty of managing data. Having a clear picture of the data sets in the organization will make it possible to establish a clear governance model.

- Organizations must also establish the data hygiene and append process. On average a B2B marketing database will go bad at a rate of 30 percent annually.[4] As this rate of decay makes clear, a process must be defined by which organizations are continually cleaning and managing data. However, only 16 percent of B2B marketing organizations are using any kind of data appending service or technology as part of their demand generation technology stack.[5] There are many vendors, such as Oceanos, and technologies such as DemandBase or ReachForce, that can provide this as an automated service. These are well worth their price because several studies show that organizations with proactive and forward-thinking data strategies outperform those without.

- Firms must also identify the various input sources of their data. Strategic demand generation is a multichannel process, and an organization will receive data from many sources by many avenues, including live events such as tradeshows, the web, telephone, list rentals, and even salespeople entering their own contacts into the CRM system. While the sources will differ, the standard by which they are used must be consistent. Demand generators need to define the minimum compliance standards for data entry. Without these standards in place, data will quickly erode and become unusable.

Developing and implementing a data governance approach is a must for B2B organizations that are looking to change outcomes of their demand generation activities. Not only will this make possible better buyer engagement and give a better overall picture of prospects, but it is also more cost effective, as numerous studies have found the cost of bad data amounts to an increase in marketing costs of anywhere between 12–15 percent annually.

Alignment of Systems to Demand Process

As demand generation data will reside in both marketing automation and CRM systems, organizations must align their systems to the demand generation process. By now it should be clear that this means mapping the systems to that of the buyers and to the Engage, Nurture, Convert buying stages. However, since many organizations are not using their technologies strategically, this presents a challenge. Regarding the buyers' continuous path to purchase, many organizations put a dividing line between marketing automation and their CRM. However, this is flawed thinking as marketing automation should have a bidirectional integration with the CRM systems and be configured so as to support the ongoing dialogue between vendor and buyer with marketing automation playing a role at enabling sales to better communicate. This approach also allows for continual monitoring and tracking of buyers' behavior, which in turn delivers very useful information to the sales rep for the time when a buyer reaches the conversion phase.

However, only slightly more than half of B2B organizations have this bidirectional synchronization between their marketing automation systems and their CRM solution.[6] This means that half of the B2B organizations are not utilizing these technologies to the fullest extent. As a result, they limit the capabilities of their technologies as well as their ability to have a full 360° view of their buyers. Perhaps this why according to SiriusDecisions, of those who own marketing automation systems, only 25 percent state they are receiving the full value from them.

Defining the Charter and Span of Control

When looking to define the approach to demand generation technologies, B2B marketing departments need to think in terms of creating a value chain model. In this model, marketing automation should be the technology at the center of the value chain because this is the technology that will automate content delivery throughout the buyers purchase path and will provide a full view into the buyers' purchase path and behavior. With marketing automation as the basis, organizations can then align other technologies, such as data appending (Engage stage), CRM (Conversion stage), and others to the buying continuum.

Moreover, organizations must define the charter for the various technologies. A technology charter is simply a document that defines the purpose and use of that technology so that there is a clear understanding of the role the specific technology will play in the execution of demand generation. Below is an example of an outline for a marketing automation platform charter that should be adopted by organizations.

- Drive limited outbound (engagement) e-mail programs and segmentation
- Manage e-mail deliverability processes and policies
- Inbound lead capture and tracking of web behavior
- Serve as a repository for all new engaged leads generated
- Manage the "nurture-able" e-mail population, execute e-mail nurturing
- Manage the lead qualification processes
- Manage the end-to-end demand generation program
- Manage the end-to-end lead-to-revenue process
- Deliver buyer insights to CRM to be used by the sales force
- Serve as a key hub for demand process analytics
- Synchronize qualified leads to the CRM system

As many marketers are still in the process of learning how to strategically utilize technology, such as marketing automation, to its fullest extent, the creation of a technology charter will bring clarity to the intended purpose of these technologies and also help set expectations about what they can deliver.

Lastly, there must be an understanding of the span of control defined for these technologies. In essence, organizations have to document who can access and activate the numerous features of their various technologies. While the use of these technologies should be widespread throughout a demand generation organization (rather than controlled by a small group of "power users"), organizations still need a hierarchy of control. This ensures that even though there are multiple users accessing the system to conduct various activities, there are controls in place to ensure the proper process is followed. When defining the span of controls, a simple way to start is defining who the system or organizational administrators of the system will be as compared to the platforms' standard users.

As mentioned earlier, technology will not deliver strategy, but ensuring that it is aligned to the demand process will allow B2B marketing organizations to develop and drive a strategy as well as empower them to receive the full value from their technology investments.

Going Beyond Marketing Automation

It is an easy temptation to think solely in terms of marketing automation and CRM as the technologies needed or used for demand generation. However, the marketing technology landscape is rapidly expanding. In his latest marketing technology supergraphic, Scott Brinker lists 43 different categories of marketing technology with marketing automation/campaign management being only one of those categories. Organizations need to give more thought to what other technologies can help improve demand generation. For starters, B2B organizations should look at a minimum of adding web analytics, data appending tools, and business intelligence solutions to their technology stack and develop a marketing technology road map so there is a clear picture of how the technology will continue to mature over the years.

Mapping Technology to Process

I have encountered only a few organizations that have mapped their technologies so as to better support their demand generation programs. To be clear, technology should support and enable the process not dictate it. B2B marketing organizations would get more value from their technology investments if they first defined their demand generation strategy and then mapped out their technologies to align to and support the strategy.

For example, I conducted the following whiteboarding exercise with a financial services organization not long ago. We mapped out the "to-be" demand generation process and then overlaid the technology stack to see how it would support the process. When we completed the mapping, we found the organization owned eight different technologies, and each one was being used in some fashion to support the organization's current demand generation practice. However, when compared to the "to-be" state, the technology stack showed multiple gaps where the use of technology needed to be expanded, and there were also redundancies. Where there were technology gaps, many on the campaign management team and field marketing were taking on manual tasks; this made them less effective and efficient. This exercise not only helped the organization crystallize its technology approach, but it helped explain some of the challenges teams faced in gaining end-to-end visibility in terms of measuring the effectiveness of demand generation. At the end of the session, the director of marketing said, "I had no idea we were using all of these systems or even what role they each played. Furthermore, we have so many gaps in our current technology infrastructure, we could not properly support our 'to-be' demand generation state." The organization has since gone to great lengths to phase out some of the duplicate systems, to integrate others, and to begin launching its first, perpetual demand generation program.

E-mail Deliverability and Best Practices

Clean data and the proper utilization of technology are essential to the success of modern, digital demand generation because so much of it depends on the use of e-mail. It is highly unlikely that B2B buyers will go through their purchase process and not include this medium. Year after year, e-mail is listed as one of the most effective ways to drive demand with 87 percent of B2B demand generators listing e-mail as their top channel for generating leads.[7] However, even clean data and the optimization of technology does not guarantee success with e-mail. The rising tide of privacy legislation, such as the newly instituted Canadian Anti-Spam Law (CASL), various compliance acts including CAN-SPAM, coupled with network filters that are designed to block certain e-mail from getting through the corporate firewall, are making it more difficult for B2B organizations to ensure that their intended messages reach their prospective buyers' in-box. To understand e-mail deliverability, marketers need to have at a minimum the details of their hard and soft bounces from their automation tool. However, those who are tasked with generating demand in their organizations need to be savvier in understanding the nuances of e-mail deliverability as well as the privacy laws that differ from one geographical region to another. A failure to understand all this will limit marketers' ability to communicate effectively with buyers, and this will lower overall lead conversion rates, impair marketing ROI, and potentially put organizations at risk of not complying with the latest regulations. Such noncompliance can lead to large fines.

For example, marketers at a large technology company told me that for three weeks they saw their conversion rates drop significantly despite having made no major changes to their demand generation programs. They finally realized they had been blacklisted (that is, their company's IP address had been identified as that of a spammer). It took this organization six weeks of work to remediate the issue, and during this time its demand generation programs suffered. As a result, the demand generation organization missed the qualified lead goals forecasted with their programs. Among the steps organizations can take to optimize their e-mail performance and ensure they are getting through to their buyers are the following:

- Whitelist their address; this is the reverse of blacklisting and means that a company's Internet protocol (IP) is recognized and approved by a particular Internet service provider (ISP). Whitelisting will enable an organization to send e-mail at a greater volume, but by itself this will not necessarily guarantee all e-mail sent will reach the in-box.
- Continually monitoring their IP address and sending domain to make sure they have not been blacklisted.
- Having a valid and up-to-date privacy policy that allows subscribers to see how their data will be protected.
- Having a dedicated IP rather than a shared IP. A shared IP address is used by several companies. As a result, if one of those companies is not following e-mail best practice, the other companies' e-mail efforts will also suffer as a result. Most marketing automation companies charge extra for a dedicated IP address, but the investment is worth it because the dedicated IP will greatly enhance e-mail deliverability.

E-mail deliverability best practices are widely discussed; yet, many B2B demand generation organizations lack the skills or knowledge to navigate these issues. Working with a Chief Privacy Officer in an organization or outsourcing this practice is something many B2B marketing teams should consider given the heavy use of e-mail in generating demand.

Data governance and an optimized technology stack are fundamental to enabling an effective demand generation strategy. Data is arguably an organization's most valuable asset when it comes to effectively driving demand; yet, it is also the area that is most often neglected. Poor data quality will not only limit demand generation performance but will cost an organization money according to Experian's estimate that the "average organization believes 23 percent of their revenue is wasted in this way."[8] B2B marketing organizations must pay closer attention to the overall health of their database and must continually fine-tune their technologies to optimize their effectiveness. Doing this with the demand process approach will greatly increase their chances of success.

CHAPTER 10

Creating an Outcome: Accountable Culture

In early 2002, while managing global marketing for a line of business at McAfee, the president of our division summoned me to his office to discuss what we were doing in marketing. I walked in and had not even sat down when he said, "Carlos, we have put a heavy investment into marketing this year to generate leads for sales. If you cannot tell me how this has benefitted the organization, I bet your replacement will." While my team had not focused on *reporting* our results to the rest of the organization, we knew we had produced positive outcomes that did benefit the business. My team and I spent the next two weeks creating spreadsheets to demonstrate the ROI we had driven for our division and documenting our results. At my next meeting the president said to me, "This is great; keep at it as I will always want you to justify marketing's existence."

While this may not be the most tactful way to motivate a team, my former boss is not unlike many CEOs and top executives who require marketing departments to "justify their existence" and show the business impact of their activities. However, as of 2013, as many as 71 percent of marketers still did not deliver the business impact their management expected.[1]

The need for B2B marketers to show business outcomes and be accountable for these outcomes is more urgent now than ever before. Recently, I spoke to colleagues at a conference about the role of marketing in B2B organizations, about how the role has changed, and about how marketing should be viewed as a growth driver within the organization. In our conversation we were trying to determine if there were other executives or departments that spend as much time justifying their budgets, fighting for more staff, or defending their role? We could not think of any, and one of my colleagues said, "This is in large part because marketing has never managed to outcomes and as a result, has not really been held accountable in delivering results to the organization at large." She was absolutely right; currently, only 25 percent of marketers can tell what marketing's impact on the business is.[2]

Part of the change that marketers need to embrace and marketing leaders need to drive is the need to manage to business outcomes and, more specifically, for demand generation to derive qualified leads that make a direct contribution to pipeline and revenue. Many CMOs I speak with are trying to ensure that their teams can consistently show their contribution to the growth of their company by having their demand generation teams focused on revenue metrics. However, while many are talking about these metrics, many are still stuck on how to move forward on this. One of the biggest limiting factors when it comes to making this change to accountability is that so many leaders miss the aspect of changing the culture; instead of just trying to change behavior, they should work on cultural change, which is the real starting point of the process.

A Culture of Change

I met with a vice president of demand generation about a year ago, and he told me that he wanted to change the role and perception of marketing in his company. One of the steps he took to help spur this change was committing the marketing organization to driving 30 percent of the corporate revenue. This was a lofty goal; while I admired his boldness, I was concerned that this stake in the ground was placed prematurely. A director in the organization told me, "We have a lot of metrics and pull them regularly, but then spend the next few weeks arguing over whether they are truly accurate; consequently, the idea of proving value never really goes anywhere." So while the goal of achieving a 30 percent contribution to revenue had been set for the team to drive change, the culture in the team had not changed. The general feeling of the team was doubt, and many in the department were fighting with each other and scared of this new objective because they felt they did not have what was needed to meet this goal.

Changing the culture in a marketing organization is paramount if the organization is to become the strategic growth driver the business needs. Many new clients tell me that "We have tried bringing in new agencies, hiring people from the outside, and developing new strategies, but change has not managed to stick." Driving a change in an organizational culture requires far more than just setting new goals, implementing a new process, or investing more money. To echo *Forbes* columnist Steve Dunning, "Changing an organization's culture is one of the most difficult leadership challenges. That's because an organization's culture comprises an interlocking set of goals, roles, processes, values, communications practices, attitudes, and assumptions. The elements fit together as a mutually reinforcing system and combine to prevent any attempt to change it. That's why single-fix changes, such as the introduction of teams, or Lean, or Agile, or Scrum, or knowledge management or some new process may appear to make progress for a while, but eventually the interlocking elements of the organizational culture take over and the change is inexorably drawn back into the existing organizational culture."[3] And this is what many marketing organizations do: they focus on one single area for change, implement one key campaign, develop a special team to address the problem, or create a new department rather than first focusing on the prevailing cultural norms and looking to change those.

Empowering People

Part of changing the marketing culture is to empower people. Marketers often tell me about the organizational roadblocks they encounter on a daily basis that prevent them from doing their jobs. One marketer confessed, "I feel like I do not have permission to do my job or to lead in the organization. Doing something different or trying to advance things to a higher level is frowned upon as it poses too much risk, and our company is definitely risk averse." While that instance may have been a view of that particular organization, many B2B marketers I meet feel the same lack of empowerment in their organizations. One of the most effective ways leaders can change their culture is to empower their people to lead in the roles and responsibilities they have. One of the mantras we have at ANNUITAS is "Lead Where You Are." We want everyone in our organization, regardless of seniority, to feel empowered. We want our employees to lead both internally and with our clients, and we seek to build a culture of leadership at every level of the organization. This is how we run our business and how CMOs need to run their departments.

Before cofounding ANNUITAS, I worked for one software company where the culture was such that marketing took a backseat to all other departments. There was plenty of talent and intelligence in the marketing department, but by and large the culture was one of apathy toward marketing. Many people there accepted the idea that the company was not benefitting from marketing in any real way and that the marketing team was not measuring outcomes to show results. On one of the weekly management calls, the vice president of marketing brought this up to the team and asked for ideas on how we, as a management team, could better empower our people and begin to change the culture of the department. The outcome of that discussion was the development of a "Take a Risk" initiative. Each employee in the marketing department was given permission to take a risk and try something new, something innovative, a calculated risk within the parameters of the person's role. The only catch was that team members had to be able to report on the results for the business, even if the results were poor, and they had to report what they learned from the risk they took. This one directive was a clear message to the marketing people that they had the permission to be bold, to break out of the prevailing order-taking culture, and to lead. As was to be expected, not all of the new initiatives taken were successful, but overall the culture began to shift and was becoming more innovative and results-oriented. The team members felt empowered to move forward and drive change. This one "Take a Risk" initiative changed the organization for the better, and the culture in the organization began to shift dramatically.

In order for transformation to succeed, marketers need to feel empowered to do the jobs they are hired to do; yet, many feel stymied in their organizations because the traditional cultural norm is to not give marketing the platform to lead. CEOs and CMOs must change this aspect in their organizations and unshackle those who are tasked with demand generation to lead effectively and drive growth for the business.

Remove the Fear and Uncertainty

"I know what I need to do, but honestly, I'm scared." This is what one marketer told me before going in front of the company's management team to present the strategic marketing plan asking for a sizeable budget to fund new initiatives. His honesty was refreshing, but the idea of someone being scared to give a presentation about the strategic initiatives and direction the company needed to go in to be successful was at the same time startling. The ideas and initiatives this marketer presented were solid and impactful and he had the business case to back them up. However, because traditionally marketing was seen as a cost center, he was afraid of trying to shatter that norm with a different approach. "Do not focus on clicks, web visits and impressions," I told him. "Focus on how these initiatives will drive revenue, increase customer retention, and increase customer acquisition. You have to act like you already have a seat at the table rather than necessarily act like you are asking for one." A few days later he reported that the presentation was received well and his team would be acting on his proposed plan. He also told me that the presentation cast marketing in a more strategic light and that the team's roles would be seen as such going forward. After this, the fear of change was gone, and he and his team were now able to move from being viewed as a cost center to being considered a growth-driver for the company.

Many marketers today live in a state of uncertainty about their roles and don't know how far they can extend their reach in the organization. This uncertainty even impacts their ability to tie their results to revenue. One reason for this fear is that marketing has never had to assume a significant role in the past.

For example, when I started my career 20 years ago, much of my time was spent focusing on branding, color schemes, product brochures, and sales enablement tools. However, today, marketing must be more strategic in an ever-changing complex environment. And the pressure is mounting as 76 percent of marketing leaders say their leadership team judges marketing success and failures faster.[4]

However, B2B marketing leaders must lead by example and show their teams that uncertainty is not an excuse any longer. If marketers are going to transform their organization, they cannot always wait until the path is free of obstacles. Carla Johnson, founder and CEO of Type A Communications, describes the dilemma marketers find themselves in as follows:

> But growth (both personal and professional) come from the courage to try new ideas, test new approaches and thinking unconventionally. That requires us to examine our perceptions about marketing's role and why we're the ideal people to spearhead change. We need to appreciate uncertainty and see its opportunity, because comfort and growth can't coexist.
>
> We can't convince executive leadership of the value we deliver to our organizations unless we believe it ourselves. Believing in ourselves and what we bring to the table is the only way that we marketers will snap out of paralysis.
>
> Because our environment has changed so dramatically many marketers feel fearful and take the safe route with their careers and their corporate initiatives. The result is a "play it safe" mentality that results in uninspired ideas and work. While we won't offend anybody, we're squandering precious opportunities to create experiences that delight our customers in new and captivating ways.[5]

Playing it safe will not help transform demand generation. The new buying environment requires marketing to take the lead in connecting with customers by approaching them in new and different ways. To some, this role may be uncomfortable, but at the same time it provides an opportunity to learn new skills and advance the careers of those who are willing. If marketing is going to accept a culture of accountability, there must be a certain freedom in the organization that empowers marketers to move forward. Eliminating fear and uncertainty in an organization will allow this to happen.

Make Them Feel Part of Something

I once worked for a midsized software company in demand generation. The organization was growing quickly, and there was a sense of excitement about the company's future. At the end of the first month I received my pay stub and noticed a line item that read "commissions." Since I was not in sales and had not closed any deals, I thought this must be some mistake. I went to my boss and pointed out the error and wanted to know how to fix the issue. My boss told me that this was not a mistake, but that everyone in the company had in some way contributed to the growth of the organization and sales, and therefore everyone received some kind of commission based on the person's role.

Of course, I was thrilled to have the additional money, but the commission also ignited in me a deep desire to do all I could to help the growth of the business, to work that much harder, and drive growth because I was fully accountable for my actions. My colleagues and I were a part of something bigger than just our marketing team, and we wanted to contribute to it in any way we could.

It is human nature to want to be a part of something; we all want to contribute, to win, to advance, and to look back over time and see that we made a difference. What is lacking in many transformation initiatives is the feeling of belonging, of real contribution. For example, I was meeting with a client going through some of the different changes that would be required in the organization when one individual put up her hands and said, "That's above my pay grade." Though the statement was met with some laughs and she was clearly speaking tongue-in-cheek, I quickly reminded her that everyone in the room had a role to play and that when we were able to launch the demand generation program and show the results, everyone in the room would also be able to celebrate the results. It's imperative that everyone engages in the necessary change as part of a team.

One of the best examples I have seen of people wanting to be part of transforming their organization is from that of one of our clients. We began working on a strategic demand generation program and our kickoff meeting was on-site at our client's office with two days of gathering data and going over our Demand Process model. The first meeting of the day included 10 people from the company, and in the course of the meeting, the discussions and interactions became more and more energetic, and the following meetings were no different.

Several weeks later when we returned to the client's office to present some of our plans and strategies for the program, our client said, "I hope it's ok, but we have a few other people from other parts of the organization who have heard about what we are doing and asked if they can sit in and be a part of the meeting." Three additional people were included in that meeting because they wanted to be a part of the transformation process. At that same meeting, the vice president of marketing asked if I could meet with the company's CEO. He had been briefed on the engagement and wanted to get a better understanding of the work we would be doing and how it would impact his company. A few weeks after that meeting, we presented our final strategy proposal to the company's executives, and by then the number of those present had grown to 20 people, all of them wanting to understand and be part of this transformation. Although this engagement and enthusiasm was important, it did not mean that changes happened overnight. However, the leadership had done a great job at spreading the word about what was taking place in the organization and at reporting on the incremental results. As a result, those who were part of the marketing organization wanted to be a part of the change that was occurring. This was the start of something powerful, and the organization is continuing to move forward and advance its transformation journey.

Measure What Counts

In order for a demand generation organization to manage to outcomes and develop a culture of accountability, there must be measurement applied to the work being done. While B2B marketers never lack for measurements on their campaigns, marketers must understand that much of what they measure is of no value to the business. The Fournaise Marketing Group routinely publishes data from its studies showing that most CEOs are largely dissatisfied with the metrics being tracked by marketers. And this is no surprise, as most marketers are still not aligning their spend, campaigns, and activity to any meaningful business metrics:

- 64 percent of marketers use "brand awareness" as their top marketing ROI KPI
- 67 percent of marketers don't believe that marketing ROI requires a financial outcome
- 63 percent of marketers do not include a financial outcome when reporting on or presenting marketing results to their CEOs and top management[6]

When I worked at BMC Software more than a decade ago, I was invited to be a part of a two-day meeting called the Metrics Summit. The goal of the two days was to bring together representatives from the various marketing groups and establish a set of common metrics for measuring the value of the various marketing activities. About 20 individuals took part in that meeting, and on the second day, our CEO walked into the conference room. The room was a picture of progress, with whiteboards covered with writing, large sticky notes on the wall that would establish common KPIs, and a presentation projected onto the screen. Upon our CEOs entrance, the discussion stopped as he said, "So this is the Metrics Summit, I'm glad to see this happening, but I have a question for all of you. Last week, we spent more than $100,000 to attend and sponsor a trade show; I would like to know what the expected return on that investment will be?" And with that, he exited the room.

His request for understanding the ROI caused quite a stir in the meeting and the representatives from the line of business that had sponsored the event together with their counterparts from the events team quickly confessed that they did not have any ROI projections and had not set up any kind of reporting on ROI. The events team representative explained, "We were there for brand recognition, not to drive leads or develop business." Another individual stated that traditionally BMC has always been at that show because it is one of the biggest of the year. Each response was an anecdotal defense of why the company had invested in the show, and each was only more proof that there was a disconnect between the marketing team and our CEO. Our CEO was not questioning whether or not we should have been at the show; he simply wanted to know the expected ROI given the large investment. This would be the same question he would ask of the sales, IT, or finance departments if they had made an equally large investment. However, marketing was unable to answer the question.

I believe there are two main reasons why marketing departments are lacking the ability to track and measure quantifiable business impact and as a result do not have a culture of accountability. The first, as mentioned earlier in this book, is a lack of training in how to manage marketing performance metrics and the analytics to interpret them, and the second is a lack of aligning measurement with the department's own goals.

This lack of skills is a major obstacle for those in B2B demand generation and is being recognized as such by Forrester Research, which found CMOs in a study reporting the following:

- 97 percent of CMOs either agree or strongly agree that "marketing must do things that it hasn't done ever before to be successful."
- 96 percent of those CMOs also state that the "breadth of skills to succeed in marketing has increased dramatically."
- 56 percent of CMOs agree that training their staff adequately is a consistent challenge.[7]

Combined with the continual changes in the buying process, pressure from the CEO to measure and report on the business analytics of marketing, and a lack of education to enable marketers to perform under these conditions, this represents a perfect storm for B2B marketers. Although many are aware of these issues, very little is being done to help stem the tide, and on average only 6.3 percent of annual B2B marketing budgets are being spent on training. And of that small percentage, only 20 percent is structured training and most (62 percent) is ad hoc.[8]

Our firm recently conducted a webinar with the e-learning division of one of the top universities on the East Coast. In planning for the event, the representative from the university remarked, "Nobody is teaching the stuff for demand generation and B2B marketing at any level. Marketers are hungry for this information as it is certainly not being taught within higher education and consulting groups are not teaching it either." While webinars and this type of education are helping B2B marketers gain knowledge that can be applied to transforming themselves and their organizations into accountable, outcome-focused environments, more must be done. Marketing and business leaders must invest in the education of their marketing personnel. It is simply not reasonable to require B2B marketers to perform tasks they are not skilled in and thus are not capable of performing. One of the most effective ways to demonstrate the belief in change and alter the culture in an organization is to invest in the people and give them the tools and education they need to succeed. Not doing so will only create a culture of frustration and disengagement and result in loss of productivity and, eventually, in a loss of revenue.

Education and training are important to an organization; however, not all of the lack of business insights and measurement skill can be blamed on a lack of knowledge. While conducting an analysis of process and applying a lens of business intelligence does require education and know-how, many marketers are simply not aligning their goals with their key measurements. In the ANNUITAS B2B Enterprise Demand Generation study, we found that almost 78 percent of marketers list "quality of leads" as their top demand generation objective. However, fewer than 20 percent of those same marketers are tracking this as a measure of demand generation success.[9] In fact, the two things most tracked by B2B marketers according to the study are "Net New Leads" and "Marketing Qualified Leads Generated." If marketers wanted to measure the success of achieving high quality of leads, they would track sales accepted and sales qualified leads as well. It is easy to see that if the demand generation metrics do not align to the goals, it will be impossible to accurately measure any impact. And this in turn will lead to more frustration and pressure from the CEO.

For example, the vice president of demand generation of a large financial services company told me they live by the "rule of 80 percent." He explained that their measurements were 80 percent accurate in terms of measuring pipeline and revenue contribution. Of course, he did not want to stay at that 80 percent accuracy level, but it was an initial goal his teams had established. The plan was that when they could consistently report and measure with 80 percent accuracy, they would increase the level to 90 percent. This executive had several reasons for taking this approach; first, the marketing department had never before measured to this level of accuracy, and if he could get his team to 80 percent, that would be far better than what they had had previously. Second, his team members were still adjusting to some of their new systems and becoming more comfortable with the changes implemented to manage to new outcomes. Third and last, he told me that 100 percent is a big goal, and if he had started with that goal, he would have only put further stress on this team. "We need to get there gradually, but make no mistake, we will get there." His plan was successful and over time his team continually focused on activity and metrics alignment and increased the accuracy of their KPIs. A few years later his team won an award for marketing excellence at an industry-wide conference, and he was able to attribute this to the department's path to transformation.

Organizational and cultural change is not an easy task, but it must be the starting point of any transformation of demand generation. The shift will take time and there will need to be continual reminders to those most impacted by the change to "trust the process." Over time, there will be a noticeable shift in thinking, in how people act, and in how they carry out their roles and responsibilities in the organization. Transformation will be realized eventually. The development of new frameworks and processes cannot come before the change in mind-set and cultural norms in the organization. In the words of famed business strategist Peter Drucker, "Culture eats strategy for breakfast." If marketing leaders can change an organization's culture, they will be well on their way to transforming demand generation and seeing improved outcomes.

CHAPTER 11

Managing People through Change

People, processes, content, and technology—these are the four major components of Demand Process. In an effort to drive change, organizations change their processes, create more content, and regularly swap out or add new people and technologies. However, what is often the most difficult to change is the attitude and perception of the people involved. I often speak with marketing leaders who discuss what they have done to enact change in their organizations. Usually, in the same breath they mention having to drag their people along "kicking and screaming." Why? Because as human beings we often see change as intimidating, scary, and volatile. Besides, B2B demand generation is morphing so rapidly that adding another layer of change that impacts how one works and operates day-to-day seems daunting at best.

For all the changes in environment, content, technology, and process that have to be made marketing leaders must first seek to win the hearts and minds of their people so that the change can become permanent. However, as the Heath brothers point out: "Often the heart and mind disagree. Fervently."[1]

About ten years into my career, I was responsible for demand generation in one of my early roles in marketing at a global software company. To help support demand generation for all the lines of business, the organization had a shared resource of an internal teleservices team whose role was to qualify leads and then route qualified leads to the sales force. This service combined cold calling to purchased lists and calling contacts who had responded to the various demand generation campaigns. After spending some time using the internal team to support my programs, I grew increasingly dissatisfied with the level of service I was receiving because the team was not producing the number of leads needed and had qualified lead conversion rates of less than one percent. My team and I spent countless hours trying to work with the teleservices people, developed call scripts for them, coached them, and worked with their management to help them improve their results, but it was all to no avail. Knowing that I needed to improve the outcomes and get more qualified leads for my sales team, I started to work toward a new solution and weighed the option of outsourcing my teleservices needs. This meant I would be shifting my budget away from the internal team, something that had never been done before. Within a few days I received a phone call from the head of the internal teleservices team asking me why I wanted to outsource this function when there were capabilities available in-house? I explained what was required of his team and that despite our best efforts, the team was not meeting the requirements, and conversion rates from qualified lead to sales accepted lead were under two percent. His response told me that his heart and his mind were at odds with each other. He told me he knew that the quality of the work was not on par with a best-in-class call center and that they were not giving me and my team what we needed. However, he explained that the members of his team were young and were really trying hard to improve and that moving this amount of business from the internal team may mean having to let a few people go. Therefore, I might want to reconsider my decision. His mind was logical in identifying the lackluster results that his team was producing, but his heart was with his team. He saw these people giving their best, and his heart and mind were providing conflicting information, making my decision to want to outsource this service very hard for him to accept.

I made the decision to continue to drive change and to continue to appeal to his mind. I also wanted his boss, the global senior vice president of sales, to be involved in the decision about the need for change because I knew I could also appeal to his mind with numbers, and he would not be so conflicted. I knew what motivated the teleservices manager's boss was reaching and surpassing quota, so if I could make the case for change via his mind and not his heart, I would get the full approval needed to outsource. Rather than try to make the case to move all of my business to an outsourced model requiring that I spend a lot of money with an unproven vendor, I proposed an experiment to run a three-month pilot with my vendor of choice with half of the business going to that source and the other half staying internal so we could do a side-by-side comparison. I knew a rational approach appealing to the mind was critical because if I tried to move all of my business to the external vendor for the pilot, the teleservices team would be impacted and that situation would involve too much of the heart. Another reason I chose this side-by-side approach was that even in appealing to the mind, it had to be a fair comparison. Had I run my pilot with all of my business outsourced, I could have potentially been compared to the internal team using metrics from a higher-performing line of business and would have been forced to stay internal. I wanted to run a fair comparison to force a cognitive decision by simply looking at the numbers. After three months, the metrics were clear: the outsourced vendor was outperforming the internal team, and I was granted approval to move all of my business outside the company. This was not an easy decision for anyone, as people were affected and this decision was something brand-new for the company, but overall, making outsourcing a decision of the mind and not the heart was key in making the change happen.

Much like the head of the teleservices team, other marketing leaders and personnel also tell me they know that what they have is broken and needs improvement but there is little being done to change existing processes and systems. They are allowing their hearts to overrule their minds, and as a result they are not transforming.

Culture Must Change Before Innovation

A few years back I met with the vice president of demand generation of a large enterprise B2B hardware manufacturer, and we discussed his company's demand generation operation. In the preceding year the firm had seen only incremental improvements in demand generation results despite a large investment in multiple channels, content marketing, and marketing automation. Clearly, he was frustrated that so little had been accomplished despite the investment and changes that had been made, and he said, "I want my team to be innovative; I want to work with vendors that are innovative. If we are going to make a difference in the organization, my team has to innovate." True, he and his team had to be more innovative. However, he was missing what many marketing leaders miss, namely, that before you can innovate, you have to change at a cultural level. You have to get the people who will drive this change to think and act differently, and this is often the biggest hurdle.

When you think about brands such as Apple, you think innovation. However, there is an understanding at Apple that this thinking, this drive to innovation, is simply part of their culture. At a Goldman Sachs conference in 2013, Apple's CEO, Tim Cook, described this culture as follows: "Innovation is so deeply embedded in Apple's culture. The boldness, ambition, belief there aren't limits, a desire to make the very best products in the world. It's the strongest ever. It's in the DNA of the company." When asked if Apple was approaching "natural limits," Cook's response was, "There's that word 'limit.' We don't have that in Apple's vocabulary."[2] There are some key words that Cook uses in his statements: "embedded," "belief," "in the DNA." Leaders at Apple have even gone so far as to remove the word "limits" from the corporate vocabulary. This culture, this belief, is now the DNA of the company, and this is why Apple has been a category creator and changer since its inception. Apple did not start on its road to success by creating innovative products; it started by building an amazing culture and getting people to buy into that culture. This then gave them the freedom to be and think in an innovative way. The rest is history.

This thought process must be embraced by those seeking to transform their demand generation operations. Demand Process is innovative, and it is different and will push the limits of traditional, tactical marketing, making some people uncomfortable. However, the change in culture is the first and most fundamental step to success.

Influencing Attitudes

Early in my career I found myself in a sales role for a small, boutique tele-marketing firm. I went to call on a prospect and upon entering his office saw a picture hanging on his wall that said "The Beatings Will Continue until Morale Improves." Hung there as more of a joke than a philosophy (I hope), the saying captures the way some organizations attempt to drive transformation in their business. This negative approach is rarely, if ever, effective and will only breed contempt in those who decide to stay in organizations that seek change in this manner.

In looking to influence the people who must achieve the needed change in an organization, marketing leaders need to focus on impacting and influencing the attitudes of their people. When I was a kid, my mother often told my siblings and me to "Change your attitude." Most of the time she was justified in this directive, but this is not something that can be done at a cognitive level and on command. I often hear marketing managers and CMOs say that their teams "just need to change their atti-tudes," as if there is an on/off switch that governs attitudes. Attitudes and beliefs are formed and influenced over time by our experiences and biases and impact the way we process information. Our attitudes influence our behavior and subsequently will have a direct correlation on our job per-formance and desire to change. We cannot simply be told to change our attitude and instantly be expected to shift behavior and thinking.

The Information Integration Theory, which was developed by Norman Anderson, sheds light on how we process information that shapes and forms our attitudes. The theory explores how attitudes are formed and changed through the integration (mixing, combining) of new informa-tion with existing cognitions or thoughts.[3] The theory assigns "value" and "weight" to all the information we receive. The value assigned to information determines whether the information itself is viewed favorably or unfavorably, and the weight is the perceived importance of the infor-mation to the one receiving it. These two factors, according to Anderson, govern how we process all the information we receive. While individual pieces of information will rarely immediately change an attitude, they will alter our views and perceptions. This means that when we receive new, positive data points about a subject toward which we have a negative attitude, the data can positively alter our attitude or perception of that subject and make it less negative. Over time, as we process or integrate more new information, the attitude can change. Anderson suggests that there are six possible ways to change an individual's attitude:

- increase the favorability (value) of a piece of existing information that supports the desired attitude
- increase the weight of a piece of existing information that supports the desired attitude
- decrease the favorability (value) of a piece of existing information that opposes the desired attitude
- decrease the weight of a piece of existing information that opposes the desired attitude
- offer a new piece of favorable information
- remind the audience about a forgotten piece of favorable information[4]

Understanding these concepts and applying them to managing the transformation of the people involved in B2B demand generation can and should radically change the way organizations present information throughout this process. For example, I worked in one marketing organization where people often said, "If you do not like the change that was just announced, wait a quarter, and it will change again." The general attitude toward change in that organization was negative, and when management sought to make another change based on new information of great importance, most employees gave it a low value., Unfortunately, any attempt at change only served to further cement negative perceptions. It is imperative that marketing leaders take the time to carefully craft their communications with their teams and shape the attitudes and perceptions of their personnel to drive greater transformation.

Look for the Bright Spots

One of the mental stumbling blocks I see most often when working with our clients on demand generation transformation is the fear of starting over. If information about the transformation is assigned a negative value by those receiving it, this will have a big impact on the overall attitude toward the initiative. People have put a lot of work and effort into what has been established (high importance), and it can be rather defeating to see this changed.

Last year I was speaking with a prospect, who has since become a client, about our approach to developing a strategic demand generation program and the work we do to develop buyer insights. One of the things our contacts pointed out was the work they had done with their internal market research team on getting to know their buyers. They had conducted market research studies, focus groups, industry studies, and had commissioned research over a two-year period to get a better view of their ideal customers. They then asked, "Are you saying that we cannot use that information?" The tone of voice alone indicated that they did not want to see their work and effort pushed aside for this change, and, although the information about transformation was very important, for some on the buying committee the thought of starting over had a negative value.

When I asked the executives to let me review the research they had completed so I could give them an answer to their question, I could see that the work they had done was impressive. During our next call I explained how we would be able to use this research and would want to replicate this type of insight. I explained to them that change does not have to, and rarely should, amount to just starting over. In fact, one of the ways to get individuals to embrace change is to identify the areas that are currently working, what the Heath brothers define as the "bright spots"[5] in the organization, and use these as a springboard for further transformation. This new information of using the work they had done was received positively and significantly improved the attitude of those in the organization who had been somewhat hesitant. Once they knew that not all of their hard work was for naught, they had a much more positive view of the work still to be done.

Looking for bright spots reinforces the value of what has already been accomplished and the advancements that have been made. When leaders recognize this and deliberately point it out, the positive perception alters the attitudes of the people who will be involved in the organizational change.

Celebrate the Wins

I am a fan of lists. I start each week by writing down the tasks in my journal that I have to accomplish that week, and as I accomplish them, I cross them off. As the week goes by, the list always grows, but there is a satisfaction I get in seeing the progress I am making toward accomplishing my tasks and goals. Tasks of lower priority get pushed into the next week, and a new set of tasks is started. Once a journal is used up, I keep it on a shelf in my office (where now I have about 20 books) to remind me of the various things I have been able to accomplish over the years. These books contain meeting notes, diagrams, etc., but they are good reminder to me that progress is being made all the time, and they serve as a reference guide for my past activities.

The same can be said for any organization that undertakes a transformation initiative. It is very healthy to look back at where you have come from and see all that has been accomplished, even if the change has not yet been fully realized. Looking back at accomplishments brings value and new, positive information to individuals and serves to remind them of that favorable information.

I saw a good example of this when I worked with a large enterprise client in the information services business. The company leaders had a giant whiteboard installed in an area of their office and had several walls covered with sticky notes and 3x5 cards taped to the wall. On my first visit there, the director of marketing took me there first. He told me that he wanted his team having visible evidence of all of the activity, change, and accomplishments they were making. On the walls were goals and strategic initiatives that had been developed; those that had been accomplished were crossed out. On other walls major accomplishments were listed, and those who had a hand in these milestones had their names and in some cases even their pictures pinned up next to the accomplishment. The director of marketing told me that he and his staff would meet every Friday in this area of the office to review the accomplishments of the week, put up new notes, and each time a team member announced the achievement of a milestone, there would be applause. He smiled as he told me "this is change in process." Later that day as I spoke to a person on his staff, I asked about the wall, and he confessed, "It's a bit cheesy, but on days when I do not think we are making much headway, I walk over there and look at all we have been able to do." The leaders were celebrating the wins, and in doing so they motivated their people. The visual display was consistently feeding people positive information, which developed and supported a positive attitude in them. It is important to celebrate the wins because adopting a Demand Process approach will not be accomplished overnight and will be hard.

One of prerequisites for this process change in any organization is defining the milestones. For example, one of our clients had identified having a marketing database of record as one of the milestones; when we announced in one of our meetings that this had been achieved, he gave a fist pump and looked at his team and said "We just made company history!" Providing the opportunity to celebrate the achievement of milestones will shape people's positive perception of the task at hand.

Don't Downplay the Change

It is vital that those who are looking to transform the way they generate demand do not try to downplay the work and effort required from their people to make this happen. Being more realistic is the only fair way to be. A colleague once challenged me after a presentation in which I had said: "Taking this new approach is not easy, but it is necessary. There will be mistakes and some failure along the way, but you need to learn from them and use these lessons to accomplish the overall goal." In his mind, I was dissuading people in the audience from embarking on any kind of initiative. He told me "People do not want to hear this stuff is hard or that there may be failure along the way. B2B marketing and demand generation is hard enough already; they want to know this is easy and that they can succeed."

In the book *Switch*, Chip and Dan Heath have this to say about failure in undertaking any change, "Any new quest, even one that is ultimately successful, is going to involve failure." They explain, "You need to create the expectation of failure—not the failure of the mission itself, but failure en route."[6] While the expectation of failure should not be necessarily be encouraged, it should not be ignored either. If this expectation is not expressed plainly up front, it can lower the morale of those involved and be detrimental to the overall goal of the change initiative.

Motivating and managing people through change is paramount to the success of any transformation initiative. The key to this is helping to shape the attitudes of those involved in the entire process. Marketing leaders cannot lose sight of this and need to know the mental temperature of their staff in order to understand what approach they need to take in disseminating information. Remember, as positive information is given and continually reinforced, attitudes toward change will improve as well.

Agile Learning

While company leaders must make sure that the people in their organization receive the right information and that this information builds and reinforces positive attitudes throughout the change process, it is of equal if not greater importance for companies to have the right people leading the change process and the transformation journey. The changes that need to occur in B2B organizations to achieve a Demand Process state are complex, span the enterprise, and are in continual motion. This dynamic requires people and leadership to be adaptable, flexible, and agile. Demand Process Transformation often fails in organizations because of the lack of these traits in the leaders responsible for the change. How can leaders identify individuals who are not ready for change? These are individuals who struggle to let go of the old ways of doing things and who are slow to respond to the complexities of new situations. For example, several years ago my team and I were working with a multibillion dollar manufacturing organization on transforming their demand generation and helping them select marketing automation. We noticed one of the individuals on the leadership team kept fighting the change. During our meetings and calls with the team, he would make statements such as, "There is a reason why we have done things this way for so long in this company," Sometimes he cast doubt on the changes that were coming by saying, "We are a large, geographically dispersed enterprise, are we sure something like this will work here?" Whatever motivated his resistance, it was clear from his statements and questions that he was not an agile leader and was slowing down the pace of change in the business.

This idea of agility in leadership has led to the concept of learning agility, and organizations that aspire to transform their demand generation operations need leaders who are learning agile, which is defined as "The willingness and ability to learn from experience and subsequently apply that learning to perform successfully under new or first-time conditions."[7] The concept of "first-time conditions" is vitally important, because the work to develop a Demand Process state will almost certainly be that. People who are agile learners are those who are eager to take on new challenges, who look to grow, and who develop and continually reflect upon experiences, and as a result they draw conclusions and learning from their experience. The Center for Creative Leadership lists five characteristics that learning agile individuals posses:

- innovating: they are not afraid to challenge the status quo
- performing: they remain calm in the face of difficulty
- reflecting: they take time to reflect on their experiences
- risking: they purposefully put themselves in challenging situations
- not defending: they are simply open to learning and resist the temptation to become defensive in the face of adversity[8]

Agile learners also tend to be "more social, creative, focused, and resilient. They are less interested in accommodating others and are not afraid to challenge norms."[9]

There is a reason why organizations want to ensure that those who are leading this transformation are agile learners or at the very least possess some of the attributes of agile learners. Throughout the process there will be adversity, and leaders will need to stay focused, be resilient, take some risks, learn from failure, and ensure they keep their eye on the goal. Considering the changes that need to happen in order to achieve a Demand Process state, this transformation will most often be a long-term proposition. Without people who possess these agile qualities leading and driving the change, it will never come to fruition. Conversely, there are leaders who display what the Center for Creative Leadership calls "derailing behavior." These are individuals who are "closed and defensive when challenged or given critical feedback."[10] Clearly, it is not optimal to put someone with this quality in a leadership position when seeking to transform demand.

For example, I know of one B2B enterprise company that started its transformation committed to transforming its demand generation operations but was unsuccessful. From the beginning, the CMO had minimal involvement in the effort and showed little support for those in the organization who were working on implementing the new approach. When the CEO asked him about the progress of the initiative, he would give little information beyond saying that his team was working on it as a "side project." There were also other leaders in the department who consistently exhibited "derailment" behavior, which means they were unwilling to change or adapt.[11] Despite the best efforts of the agile learners who were looking to drive the change in pockets of the organization, the resistance of the derailing individuals and the lack of input or involvement from the CMO led to no real change at all. Those who wanted to see the changes ended up leaving the organization. They realized that what they hoped to achieve could never be accomplished in such a dysfunctional organization (this is the reflective attribute). This is to say that in most organization there will be individuals who try to derail the change process because of their inability to change, but in this particular instance the derailing behavior was particularly prominent and led by the CMO and thus prevailed over those who were hoping to improve the company's demand generation maturity.

Demand Process Transformation in organizations of any size is not a goal that is easily achieved. This is because people are greatly impacted by change and people are the most important part of the equation. Ensuring that those who are a part of and leading this transformation are open to and embrace the change will be key to ensuring a successful initiative. On the other hand, people who are closed to and resist change will make this process more difficult and will at times succeed in stopping the transformation. It is not enough to have the people with the right skills to drive the change, it is important to have people with the right skills combined with the needed mental makeup that will see the goals of transformation become a reality. This is a tall order, but the success of change will not be achieved without it.

CHAPTER 12

The Need for Change

The need for change in B2B demand generation cannot be ignored any longer, but yet for many organizations the question still is how to manage change. There are three fundamental reasons why B2B marketing leaders need to embrace change—our buyers require it, our organizations need it, and never before have demand generation professionals been better equipped to do it.

The Buyers' Requirements

There is no question that the purchase path of modern B2B buyers has been the catalyst to the upheaval that has occurred in B2B marketing and the driving force behind the impetus for change. Buyers now have one-click access to all the information they need to make informed buying decisions, all in the palm of their hand. As a result, they now control when they will engage with a vendor to advance their purchase. As controllers of their own purchase destiny, buyers are demanding a more personalized, logical, and relevant response from vendors in terms of content, and they require a dialogue with vendors. Yet many B2B marketers are struggling to make this happen, as evidenced by the majority of marketing departments that despite their increased investment in demand generation and content creation are still not seeing the expected value or improvement.

While the B2B buying process has changed, by and large, B2B buyers still want to make smart purchase decisions and align with a vendor they can trust. And demand generation content must speak to these needs and also be packaged in a way that buyers can and want to consume. In the DemandGen Report 2015 Content Preferences Survey, the two highest rating content types that buyers prefer are foundational and prescriptive content.[1] Foundational content is described as blueprints or toolkits that help buyers prepare for their purchase. An example of this type of content would be an request for proposals (RFP) template or a selection guide. Prescriptive content is described as content that details steps or how-to content.

In addition to detailing the content type, buyers have also indicated that they want interactive, digestible content that is supported by data and is easy to access.[2] While this type of content is beginning to emerge from leading companies, it is still not common in many demand generation programs. Even when this kind of content is offered, it is often presented in a one- and-done, tactical style that does not in any way continue the dialogue with buyers.

Our buyers also want a better web experience, but many B2B vendors are missing the mark there as well. When asked what content was missing from vendor websites, B2B buyers listed case studies, articles, and white papers as the content that was most often missing followed by pricing information as the second kind of information that was missing most often. Moreover, 68 percent of buyers indicated they wanted vendor contact information but had difficulty finding it.[3] Giving buyers every opportunity to connect and initiate contact with a vendor is foundational to demand generation. If buyers have to work to find contact details on a vendor's website, they will likely abandon the site and go elsewhere. If contacting a vendor is difficult during the buying process, buyers will begin to wonder if this difficulty will persist after their purchase when they are customers.

One of the goals of demand generation is to educate buyers during the purchase process so they can make a more informed buying decision. Yet, according to the data collected from buyers—and based on what I hear from buyers I interview on behalf of clients—this kind of educational content is often lacking.

I was meeting with one of our clients recently and evaluating the content required for the client's demand generation program. One of the approaches for this program was to build a "resource center" on the client's corporate website that would allow buyers to come in and select content based on their persona. Based on that selection, the website would dynamically deliver the content. In order to build on this approach, we met with the client's corporate web team to get more details on what was needed and discuss the changes that needed to be made to the corporate website. During the meeting, the web team voiced opposition to taking this approach. The team members discussed the difficulty of developing dynamic pages, questioned the data we had collected from the buyers, and resisted changing the form and structure of their website. Despite the fact that we had research and verbatim feedback from customers and prospects to support our position, the change was a difficult one for the team to embrace. If the team had prevailed with this resistance, the company's buyers would still not have access to the kind of content they desired. Had it not been for the insistence of the rest of the individuals involved in the engagement, the work would never have been completed.

Our buyers are taking a different approach to their purchasing and have formed new buying habits. As they are firmly in control, they require vendors (both marketing and sales teams) to follow suit and to adapt and transform how they interact with buyers during their purchase journey.

There is no better reason for B2B organizations to initiate the needed change in the approach to demand generation than meeting the buyers' needs, and, in reality, there is no other choice for B2B companies. When I asked Robert Rose of the Content Marketing Institute what the risk was for organizations that do not adapt, he was quick to respond: "You die, it's just that simple. It may not happen tomorrow, but it will happen."[4] While that may seem extreme, there are plenty of examples on the retail side showing the death that comes to an organization when it does not adapt or change based on the customers' needs. Would anyone have thought 15 years ago that Blockbuster Video and Borders Books would go out of business? Those companies missed the opportunity to respond to the demands of their buyers and suffered a slow corporate death. B2B organizations will suffer the same fate if they do not begin to meet the buyers where they are and deliver a well-connected, end-to-end buying experience.

What CEOs Want

As mentioned in preceding chapters, there is currently an uneasy truce between CEOs and their CMOs. The main driver behind this lack of trust is that most CEOs believe that CMOs are too disconnected from the realities of the company. I see this disconnect from those in marketing leadership roles in the companies we work with and speak to. I recently reviewed the marketing report that had been prepared for a company's executives with one of the firm's marketing executives. This organization had made a large investment in demand generation and technology resulting in many new initiatives being launched. With the flurry of activity that came from the renewed focus on marketing, expectations were high that marketing would be able to become a growth driver for the business. However, when looking at the details of the presentation, we saw that there were no quantifiable metrics indicating the value the organization received from the investments. The marketing team had tracked the increase of visitors to the company's website, the number of leads routed to the sales force, the number of events, webinars, new content, and so on. The marketing people had done a great job of describing the activity but failed to connect the dots of all this activity to pipeline, revenue, and any quantifiable impact on the business.

Many things can keep CEOs awake at night, but ultimately their focus and goal is to maximize margin, enhance the customer experience, and increase revenue and margins. The CMO should have this same focus, and in fact, more and more CEOs want to know what steps the CMOs and their marketing teams are taking to make this happen. I speak to many CMOs and marketing executives who desire to have a seat at the executive table. They talk about being shut out, being kept at bay, or not having a strong enough voice in the company to drive real change. Perhaps the reason for this is that they lack a common language. Marketing executives too often speak a language that is different from the one used by the other executives at the table; specifically, marketing executives often lack solid financial metrics that show their contribution to the company's revenue. Until marketing executives can demonstrate their business value, the fact that they are a strategic part of the organization will go unnoticed.

Sales Needs Help

With B2B buyers waiting longer and longer in their purchase journey to engage with sales representatives, it is up to marketing to fill the gap that sales once owned. Very few B2B marketers are doing this with any real success as evidenced by the 2.8 percent who say they are not highly effective in meeting their demand generation goals. Marketing must also lead in training sales people in this new buying paradigm. Part of this training is educating sales teams on the demand generation program and on how to continue the dialogue with the buyer. Additionally, marketing needs to educate sales on the insights into buyers and how to translate these insights into key talking points. When marketing leads by enabling sales and delivering highly qualified leads for the sales team, greater alignment results. For example, in one organization I know of the head of demand generation regularly receives e-mails from the sales force thanking the marketing people for the quality leads and asking the demand generation team to provide more training for sales.

It is no longer a sales-driven world and it is incumbent on marketers to step up to the challenge and help the sales team understand that they can still be an integral part of the conversation, but that the tone and approach has to change in order for them to participate in today's buying discussion.

I was talking on the phone with a colleague who sells for a software company and is getting pressure from his upper management because a few deals have slipped. He sells to large enterprise organizations, and often they are slow to make decisions; they are rife with buying committees and require involvement of the procurement department. He has been told to just issue a proposal and invite the potential buyers to a meeting; his managers think this will help drive the sale. This approach does not work, however, as buyers will not be strong-armed into making a deal.

Our businesses leaders are begging for B2B demand generation to change, and sales teams need the marketing department to take a leadership role in connecting with buyers and help the sales force adapt and win. This is not a question of *if* this is needed but of *when* it will happen. And the time for Demand Process Transformation is now.

There Is No Better Time!

I remember many times during my career looking at multiple spreadsheets and trying to calculate the ROI of our marketing programs. I would wonder just how accurate these manually generated reports actually were. I remember when the sales team was the primary customer of marketing, and the main job of my team was to supply the salespeople with what they felt they needed to be successful in the field. At that time only limited technology was available, and the lack of data and analytics meant that marketing was more an art than a science. However, all of that has radically changed, and today's B2B marketers have more tools, access to insights, and a bigger budget at their disposal than ever before. Despite all this, I meet more B2B marketers who feel discouraged, unfulfilled in their profession, and unsure about whether they should just abandon ship and look for a different career path. On the contrary! I cannot think of a more exciting or opportune time to be a B2B marketer. Very few people ever have a chance to do great things in their career and demonstrate the value they bring to their organizations on a day-to-day basis. I think of B2B marketing professionals I follow and for whom I have great respect: Megan Eisenberg, CMO at Mongo DB; Nick Panayi, head of digital marketing and global brand at CSC; Lisa Horner, SDR channel director at appfolio; Brian Kardon, CMO of Lattice Engines. They and many others have embraced the new role of marketing, changed their organizations significantly, and moved marketing into strategic roles. These individuals are examples of what great marketers can do when change is embraced and when they transform their organizations, starting with the culture, into business growth engines. These individuals are also examples of why B2B marketers should get excited about the opportunity that lies ahead for this profession. The time for B2B marketers is now, and the only thing that can stand in the way of making great changes happen is our own reluctance. Will there be obstacles and challenges along the way? Absolutely! But the same can be said for any job. As one individual I recently spoke to put it, "I know I am in a little bit over my head, but I am excited for the challenge and cannot wait to see us accomplish some great things!" This is the type of approach to embrace; this is the time for B2B marketers to make a difference; this is the era when marketers can transform and drive quantitative demand and play a strategic role in the growth of organizations.

CHAPTER 13

Change Ahead

For all of the turmoil and change B2B marketing has seen for a number of years now, there is still more to come. Forrester surveyed 117 marketing executives and 96 percent of them either agreed or strongly agreed that "The pace of change in technology and marketing will continue to accelerate."[1] In essence, we are still in the early stages of what lies ahead in this age of modern marketing.

As a result, the complexity of B2B demand generation will continue to grow as buyers will continue to add sophistication to their approaches to purchase, their time frame to connect with vendors will elongate, and buying committees will continue to expand when making strategic purchases for their organizations.

IDCs Kathleen Schaub recently published her "10 Predictions for the Next Three Years." They were as follows:

1. 25 percent of CMOs will be replaced every year through 2018.
2. By 2017, 25 percent of marketing organizations will solve critical skill gaps by deploying centers of excellence.
3. By 2017, 15 percent of B2B companies will use more than 20 data sources to personalize a high-value customer journey.
4. By 2015, one in three marketing organizations will deliver compelling content at all stages of the buyer journey.
5. In 2015 only one in five companies will retool to reach line-of-business buyers and outperform those selling exclusively to IT.

6. By 2017, 50 percent of larger high-tech marketing organizations will create in-house creative services.

7. By 2018, 20 percent of B2B sales teams will go "virtual," resulting in improved pipeline conversion rates.

8. By 2017, 70 percent of B2B mobile customer apps will fail to achieve ROI because they lack customer value-added.

9. By 2017, 25 percent of CMOs and CIOs will have a shared road map for marketing technology.

10. By 2018, 20 percent of B2B CMOs will drive budget increases by attributing campaign results to revenue performance.[2]

If you look at these predictions by IDC, all of them have an impact on either the people, process, content, technology, or measurement of marketing. The changes are happening in real time at buyer, organizational, data, and technology levels; B2B marketers need to understand the impact these changes are having on their roles and their ability to execute the mandate to drive demand.

In an interview one of the leading analysts in the B2B marketing and sales space said, "I would not say nothing has changed, but it certainly has not changed in the way you would think it would have given the awareness of the problem and the technology available to solve the problem."[3] While there have been some incremental changes in B2B marketing and demand generation practices, the transformational Demand Process change—change that is needed to stay ahead of the buyer and drive the necessary results commensurate with the large investments being made—has not yet happened. Much of this has been due the fact that marketers have underestimated the problem and succumbed to the belief that these challenges could be addressed in a technology-driven, tactical fashion. Regarding this point, the analyst said, "This has also led to the slow growth—nobody has had the gumption to say this is a difficult problem to solve—technology lured us into thinking that this was a solution; you could see more leads, more impact to pipeline, more movement on customer behavior, but the issue is to do it again while measuring the impact, and that's where you hit a wall."[4] And it is this wall that marketers must scale.

The Benefits of Change

Throughout this book, I have written about the changes that need to occur to drive demand and deliver a better buying experience for prospects and customers. In my interactions with many B2B marketing leaders, the one common question they asked is "Is it worth it?" This is a great question, as it indicates not reluctance but rather the fact that these leaders understand the enormity of the task of transforming their organizations at every level. The short answer is yes. It is not easy, but it is worth it. As we work with our clients at ANNUITAS, we speak about a Demand Process Maturity Model (figure 13.1); this is a model that was developed by our chief strategy officer, Adam Needles, to show organizations the path to transformational maturity.

Each phase in the maturity model has a governance level and forecasted conversion rates, and each can be summarized as follows:

- *Stage 0*
  - *Governance Level:* No end-to-end documentation of overall demand generation process with a tactical, activity-based approach to demand generation

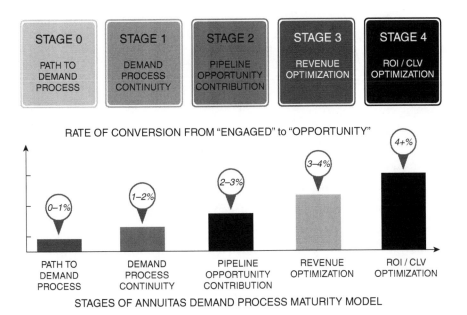

Figure 13.1 ANNUITAS Demand Process Maturity Model.

- *Engaged to Opportunity Conversion Rate:* 0–1 percent
- *Maturity Summary:* Lack of overall process with disjointed approach to demand generation. Primary focus of Engagement and Conversion with little to no Nurturing

- *Stage 1*
  - *Governance Level:* End-to-end process documentation
  - *Engaged to Opportunity Conversion Rate:* 1–2 percent
  - *Maturity Summary:* Initial Demand Process concepts, with basic lead-to-revenue and closed-loop management of the buyers state with a basic layer of Engagement, Nurture, and Conversion

- *Stage 2*
  - *Governance Level:* Best practice process standards with lead-stage conversion governance
  - *Engaged to Opportunity Conversion Rate:* 2–3 percent
  - *Maturity Summary:* A focus on improving conversion rates in lead stage by optimizing content offers. Conducting initial program and buyer funnel optimization by fine-tuning the program content offers, scoring, and logic by lead stage.

- *Stage 3*
  - *Governance Level:* Continual process optimization and content and behavioral model governance
  - *Engaged to Opportunity Conversion Rate:* 3–4 percent
  - *Maturity Summary:* Moving to a state of precision on revenue delivery from demand generation programs with deeper analytics applied to demand generation programs. Improvement in lead velocity and time to revenue through optimizing the buyer experience.

- Stage 4
  - *Governance Level:* Predictive demand generation process with account and high value management governance
  - *Engaged to Opportunity Conversion Rate:* 4 percent and higher
  - *Maturity Summary:* Program fine-tuning and optimization is focused on maximizing ROI and customer lifetime value. Demand generation is viewed as an investment, not as a cost. Optimizing the account level experience via an initial focus on predictive modeling.

Most of the organizations I encounter fall somewhere between Stage 0 and Stage 2 in their Demand Process maturity and have been there for some time. To get an understanding of where your organization is in terms Demand Process maturity it is important to analyze every part of the Demand Process: people, processes, content, and technology. The following questions can help you make the assessment:

- People:
  - What is the state of collaboration between marketing and sales teams?
  - What are the defined roles of marketing and sales teams regarding demand generation?
  - Are there clear SLAs between marketing and sales departments?
  - Does the sales team appropriately follow up on qualified leads? (appropriate would be within 48 hours)
  - How does the structure of the marketing organization hurt or help sales alignment?
- Processes:
  - Is there a clear definition of a qualified lead?
  - Do the lead definitions map to an ideal customer profile or persona?
  - Is there a clearly defined lead-to-revenue process that has been documented?
  - Are there defined routing rules to ensure qualified leads are sent to the sales team in a timely manner?
  - Do marketing and sales teams work with one set of metrics across the funnel and agree on ideal conversion stages?
  - Is there an established target for the percentage of marketing's revenue contribution to the pipeline? What are the obstacles to achieving this?
- Buyer insights and content
  - Is mapping the buying process and defining the buyer dialogue a part of the demand generation program's design?
  - Are there specific content offers to cover every stage of your targeted buyer's journey as part of your demand generation strategy?

- Is there a multichannel (both inbound and outbound) approach to your demand generation? What is the current mix of inbound and outbound channels?
- Is nurturing part of your holistic demand generation strategy or is it treated as a separate campaign?
- Are sales teams involved in developing the demand generation strategy?
- Do the demand generation programs focus on new customer acquisition and on cross-selling and retention of your current customer base? (Demand generation should be designed for both purposes.)
- Technology systems and data
  - Do data and technology enable closed-loop demand generation?
  - Do you have the right systems for the execution of strategic demand generation?
  - What are the other major systems that play a role in demand generation and how are they contributing?
  - What is the state of marketing, sales, and executive dashboards for marketing programs?
  - Is there data governance within the organization to ensure data integrity?
- KPIs
  - What are the top goals and objectives of the demand generation programs and do the current KPIs track the success?
  - What lead-to-revenue process metrics are measured?
  - How confident are you that you can impact demand generation KPIs with targeted programs and investments?
  - Do sales and marketing teams have established KPIs that both departments measure to drive demand process alignment?
  - Do the KPIs track marketing's contribution to pipeline and revenue?

By bringing together the marketing and sales teams to walk through these questions and getting honest feedback, organizations will shed light on some of their issues, identify the cause of these problems, and can then begin to determine the course of action they need to take to optimize their demand generation programs and improve the value of marketing investments. Any organization that is lower than a stage 3 maturity needs to consider making organization-wide changes as this low maturity level indicates a lack of a strategic approach to generating demand.

One organization that my firm, ANNUITAS, has had the privilege to work with went through a similar type of assessment, and the company determined that it needed to transform its approach to connecting with their buyers. The improvements people in that company have made over time have been significant, and the marketing team is now making a real impact on the business and has changed from a cost center to a growth driver for the business. I have included that company's story here in the hope that those who are asking whether the change is worth it will get their answer.

Lenox Case Study

LENOX, a division of Newell-Rubbermaid Inc., started in 1915 with 10 employees and a passion for bringing customers industrial saw blades that cut faster and lasted longer. In business for nearly 100 years, the passion hasn't changed—but the team has grown to more than 900 people who manufacture and market the LENOX products in more than 70 countries.

The Challenge

As one of the world's leading providers of industrial saw blades, LENOX has been successfully selling top-quality metal cutting products for nearly a century. But a winning track record in the market doesn't guarantee optimized marketing results.

With revenue growth and market share viewed as ongoing priorities by the company's leadership, the LENOX marketing team wanted to keep winning new customers and to demonstrate value to its broad base of stakeholders—mill owners, plant executives, office and "on-the-floor" personnel as well as other potential targets.

The challenge, however, was twofold. First, LENOX realized the ways its target base received information and consumed relevant content were changing. And second, marketing's primary focus was on getting products launched and promoted, not on tracking leads. As a result, the demand generation process was saddled with inefficiencies, and there were no clear metrics for reporting—and validating—results.

The Solution

LENOX looked to transform its traditional approach and build a buyer-centric demand generation strategy—one that would lay the foundation for the most profitable lead conversion program in the company's history. And in less than 12 months, that's just what LENOX did.

The process began by developing buyer insights through in-depth customer and industry-based research designed to identify the personas and primary pain points of key decision makers. Through this process it was determined that, historically, the company's demand generation strategies didn't match the buyers' journey. In particular, LENOX lacked materials and communications to continue the conversation with potential buyers during intermediate stages. As a result, many potential buyers lost interest before they were ready to act.

As part of the strategic demand generation program, LENOX created the Industrial Metal Cutting Resource Center as part of the corporate website. The center's content meets the needs of potential customers regardless of where they are in the buying cycle. Basic information on metal cutting operations drives engagement and establishes LENOX as a reliable resource for critical metal cutting information. The center also includes educational sections on how to improve performance along with LENOX product information and trial and demo options.

Leads are also nurtured by maintaining a steady flow of content-driven communications. Blogs, SEO, PPC, list rentals, benchmarking studies, industry white papers, marketing automation, and other tactics keep LENOX in front of potential buyers. Instead of targeting buyers with a random flow of content, LENOX engages potential customers through ongoing conversations appropriate for every stage of the buying journey.

Based on what specific content potential buyers choose to download, the system captures where buyers are in their own decision-making process. The resulting leads are then given weighted scores and categorized from engagement to warm leads to hot leads.

Qualified leads are turned over to the sales team and managed proactively via a framework jointly developed by the LENOX sales and marketing departments. As a result, sales and marketing are both driving greater ROI.

The Result

LENOX increased marketing's contribution to the sales pipeline from the single digits to nearly 10 percent for 2014—doubling the previous system's tally. And today, the demand generation engine consistently converts 11.21 percent of engaged leads into hot leads for the sales organization.

Prepare for Adversity

As with any initiative to do things differently, there will be challenges and adversity along the way and some people will balk at the level of discomfort the transformation will bring. Others, for various reasons, will look to stop the change or not embrace it fully. Some plans will fail, and at times there will be a disheartening feeling of taking two steps forward and three back. This is commonplace and should be expected from the outset. Transformation and change management is hard work and should not be taken lightly or undertaken with the thought that it will be simple. I know of two companies, a large enterprise financial services company and a large enterprise software firm, that both set out to transform their demand generation approach; both are in the third year of this transformation (as planned and expected) and are still undergoing the process of change. This change is a long-term proposition and should be recognized as such while wins along the way should also be highlighted.

Demand Process Transformation requires strong leadership and those who see it through will reap the rewards and become a strategic player in the day-to-day operations of their business and will contribute greatly to corporate growth.

Start Small, Dream Big, Scale Appropriately

As detailed earlier, a change this broad and expansive cannot be completed quickly in an enterprise organization. Changing culture, processes, frameworks, content, and technology is an enormous undertaking, but it can be done with an understanding of the overall vision; it needs planning for the execution and starting with a minimally disruptive approach that both tests and proves the new model.

The landscape of B2B marketing is undergoing continual change, which necessitates a new way for organizations to drive demand. This has to be done in a holistic manner, and the companies that are successful will realize that as much as this is about adapting the approach of people, processes, content, and technology, this process is about realizing that this transformation is a change management initiative that will require thinking differently and a change in the prevailing cultural norms. In talking about the cultural aspects of change, Sheryl Adkins-Green, CMO of Mary Kay, says, "Culture connects employees to a company and its mission. This connection can make or break a strategic plan."[5] Many CMOs are missing the all-important element of change management as they seek to move their organizations to respond to the modern buyer and in so doing are limiting the success of their demand generation programs and marketing as a strategic business partner.

This book provides the information on how to change the people, processes, content, and technology in order to effectively drive demand, maximize budget, optimize technology and resources, and have a greater impact on business and better alignment with B2B buyers. If organizations are going to achieve a modern state of demand generation, there has to be a fundamental understanding that it is all about change management. It is time for B2B CMOs to lead this transformation in their organizations and inspire their people to do the same and in so doing realize the benefits of Demand Process.

CHAPTER 14

Demand Process Glossary

Throughout this book terms have been used that are not necessarily common in the B2B demand generation vocabulary. Having an understanding of these terms will help as you, the reader, apply the concepts that have been detailed in this book and aid you in changing the approach your organization takes to demand generation. Below is a glossary of terms that will serve as a reference as your organization begins the journey toward change management and Demand Process Transformation.

Active Interest Threshold (AIT)

A component of the lead scoring model, this defines the minimal level of interaction buyers must maintain to stay active in the program. This factor becomes useful in "holding back" buyers who may have gone cold and are not considered qualified leads even though they have a long history of interactions.

By using decaying interest factors, such as lapses in activity, marketers can reduce the active interest threshold and thus "pull the buyer back" from advancing to the next lead qualification stage unless new activity is detected.

Attributed Revenue Per Content Offer

Total revenue attributed to download of the content offer (unweighted).

Buyer Dialogue Logic

The translation of the buying process stages into the discrete information requests buyers have as they advance from one buying process stage to the next—from initial pain point to final solution. This defines the detailed conversation the company wishes to have with buyers from engagement all the way through to conversion—across both marketing and sales interactions.

Once the buyer dialogue logic is defined, it serves as the critical organizing thread for the demand generation program, upon which all content marketing, lead management, and organizational and technology layers should be built.

Catalyst Content

This is Engagement content in offers that are designed to align with a specific, higher-order buyer pain point. Often, this is offered when a buyer is right at the point of "getting off the fence" and beginning the active buying process.

Catalyst content is the type of content offer that is leveraged at the active engagement content offer stage.

Content Marketing Model

The core management framework for the dialogue with B2B buyers. It defines all of the potential content offers and sequencing required to drive buyers forward in their buying process. The goal of content marketing is to orchestrate the delivery of the right content to the right buyer, in the right place, at the right time.

Accomplishing this requires analysis of the buying process and of the buyers' content consumption as they move through a decision-making process; insights from this process must be matched to content categories, topics, and themes, and then must be integrated with touchpoints across multiple digital media. In this way content marketing represents both the buyer-facing management framework and our strategic approach to educating and adding continuous value throughout the buying process.

Content Offer (CO)

Any content piece—whether whitepaper, video, etc.—designed to address a specific information request buyers have in their buying process. Typically, there are multiple content offers developed per information request stage within the buyer dialogue logic thread.

Content Offer Cost

Production cost per content offer.

Content Offer Downloads Per Content Offer

Total number of downloads per content offer.

Content Offer Submit Rate Per Content Offer

Conversion rate from impression to download per content offer.

Conversation Track

A common path for a single or multiple personas from pain point to solution. Typically, a group of personas will be distilled down into several common conversation tracks, and then content offers will be designed to shape the conversation track from the information request stage to a stage within the Buyer Dialogue Logic. Note that there will typically be one buyer dialogue logic but multiple conversation tracks aligned to this buyer dialogue logic.

Convert

A holistic demand process stage; this is the third stage in the progression from Engage to Nurture to Convert that moves buyers from automated inbound/outbound content offers to live sales interactions and sales education stages. At the same time the lead is advanced to a qualified lead and then to a sales-ready lead, from opportunity to closed-won or closed-lost deal. Conversion leverages profiling and scoring to escalate the dialogue at the right time, identifying and driving purchase behavior.

Cost Per Attributed Revenue Per Content Offer

Average cost per $1 of revenue per content offer (unweighted).

D-CO (Drip Content Offer)

This is content that is delivered in a periodic and perpetual stream when buyers have not responded to nurturing or to attempts to reengage; drip content offers help to stay "top of mind," and interaction with this content provides the scoring and logic basis to reinsert buyers into an active nurturing track. A string of D-COs is a drip track. The content of D-COs typically focuses on thought leadership.

Demand Generation Center of Excellence (DGCoE)

A demand generation center of excellence model defines a company's organizational approach to managing the Demand Process. It considers the stakeholders involved in driving specific demand generation programs and in optimizing the overall Demand Process from the standpoints of process, content, and technology. This center of excellence identifies how these key stakeholders should interact, and it examines this both from a functional/discipline (e.g., web or marketing operations) standpoint and from a Demand Process standpoint (e.g., responsibility for inbound engagement).

For a large enterprise organization, a demand generation center of excellence model should not be centralized; rather, it should be distributed/hybridized—that is, some elements should be centralized but others should be pushed out to the "front lines." Thus the demand generation center of excellence model helps provide overall governance and sets standards for how demand generation activities can be better orchestrated and work together in a closed-loop, optimizeable manner.

Demand Chain Management

The ability to manage demand and revenues as strategically and holistically as companies manage their supply chain and costs.

Demand Generation "Plays"

Demand generation programs must be aligned to some defining unit. One way to do this is to follow the concept of a "sales play"—i.e., the major types of interaction, aligned to a buyer pain point; this is what leads a company to initiate interaction with a new buyer. Sales plays are aligned to solution categories; demand generation "plays" are an alignment of demand generation programs to the buyer mind-set.

Demand Generation Programs

The fundamental, perpetual building block for an overall Demand Process. A demand generation program is an always on, perpetual set of interactions, organized around a common buyer dialogue logic, typically spanning several conversation tracks and multiple personas. The program is composed of a buyer dialogue logic, content marketing model, lead management framework, and a Demand Process integration scheme. The defining element of a demand generation program is typically a holistic "sales play" or major solution or product area.

Engaged Per Channel

Number of resultant "engaged" buyers in the lead qualification stage. Analyzed per engagement channel (e.g., list rental vs. PPC).

Lead Stage Velocity Per Content Offer

Average time between download of the content offer and the buyer reaching a given lead qualification stage.

Prospect Impressions Per Channel

Number of potential touch points for an engagement content offer (i.e., impressions) with prospects, whether the prospect chose to download the content offer or not. Analyzed per engagement channel (e.g., list rental vs. PPC).

Prospect To Engaged Conversion Ratio Per Channel

Percent conversion rate from prospect impression count to engaged buyer count. Analyzed per engagement channel (e.g., list rental vs. PPC).

Notes

Introduction

1. Cooperstein, D. (2012, July 11), "Marketing Change Management: Like It Or Not, You Have To Figure It Out," *Forbes,* http://www.forbes.com/sites /davidcooperstein/2012/07/11/marketing-change-management-like-it-or-not -you-have-to-figure-it-out/.
2. Throughout this book, I will use B2B as abbreviation of business-to-business.
3. Content Marketing Institute (2015), *B2B Content Marketing Benchmarks, Budgets & Trends.* http://contentmarketinginstitute.com/wp-content/uploads/2014/10 /2015_B2B_Research.pdf.

1   The Issues with Modern Demand Generation

1. ANNUITAS (2014), *Enterprise B2B Demand Generation Study.* Atlanta, GA.
2. CEB (2015), *Unlock Your Potential in 2015*: *CEB Sales, Service, Marketing, Communication.* Arlington, VA.
3. ANNUITAS website.
4. McLellan, L. (2012, January 03), "By 2017 the CMO will Spend More on IT Than the CIO," Gartner High Tech Webinar Series, http://my.gartner.com /portal/server.pt?open=512&objID=202&mode=2&PageID=5553&resId=1871 515&ref=Webinar-Calendar.
5. Brinker, S. (2015, January), "Marketing Technology Landscape Supergraphic," http://cdn.chiefmartec.com/wp-content/uploads/2015/01/marketing_technology _jan2015.png.
6. DemandGen Report (2013), *2013 B2B Content Preferences Survey.* Hasbrouk Heights, NJ.
7. Rose, R. (2014, September 22), Chief Strategy Officer, Content Marketing Institute, C. Hidalgo, interviewer, Colorado Springs, CO.
8. Ramos, Laura (2013), *B2B CMOs Must Evolve or Move On.* Cambridge, MA: Forrester.
9. Ibid.
10. Ibid.

2   Leading Demand Process Transformation

1. CEB (2012), *The Digital Evolution in B2B Marketing*, http://www.executive board.com/exbd-resources/content/digital-evolution/pdf/Digital-Evolution-in -B2B-Marketing.pdf.

3   Why Transformation Fails

1. eMarketer (2014, May 22), *Skills of the Modern Marketer Report*.
2. Needles, A. (2013, August 28), "Is the CMO the Problem?" in *DemandGenReport*, http://www.demandgenreport.com/industry-topics/demanding-views/2296-is -the-cmo-the-problem.html.
3. Panayi, N. (2014, November, 5), head of digital marketing and global brand at CSC, C. Hidalgo, interviewer, Colorado Springs, CO.
4. Industry analyst (2013, November 19), C. Hidalgo, interviewer, San Francisco, CA.

4   Action Does Not Equal Change

1. Regalix Research (2015), *State of B2B Marketing 2015.* http://www.regalix.com /by_regalix/research/reports/state-of-b2b-marketing-2015/.
2. Content Marketing Institute (2015), *B2B Content Marketing Benchmarks, Budgets & Trends.* http://contentmarketinginstitute.com/wp-content/uploads/2014/10/2015 _B2B_Research.pdf.
3. ANNUITAS (2014), *Enterprise B2B Demand Generation Study.* Atlanta, GA.
4. David Raab (2014), *Raab VEST Report.* http://raabguide.com/vest.
5. Ibid.
6. Ibid.
7. Ibid.
8. Ibid.

5   Changing the Marketing and Sales Mind-set

1. Industry analyst (2013, November 19), C. Hidalgo, interviewer, San Francisco, CA.
2. DemandGen Report (2015), *DemandGen Report Benchmark Study: What's Working in B2B Demand Generation.* Hasbrouk Heights, NJ.
3. ANNUITAS (2014), *Enterprise B2B Demand Generation Study.* Atlanta, GA.
4. *Forbes* (2013, May 08), "What is Social Selling? Connections and Content," http:// www.forbes.com/sites/sap/2013/05/08/what-is-social-selling-connections-and -content/.
5. Fournaise Marketing Group (2012, July 10), "80% of CEOs Do Not Really Trust Marketers ('Except If They Are "ROI Marketers')," https://www.four naisegroup.com/ceos-do-not-trust-marketers/.
6. van Meurs, B. (2014, April), senior vice president and CMO for imaging systems at Phillips Healthcare. "CMO Lessons in Working with A CEO," T. French, interviewer.

7. Accenture (2013), "The CMO-CIO Disconnect: Bridging the Gap to Seize the Digital Opportunity."
8. Ibid.
9. ITSMA (2013), "Realizing the Promise of Marketing Technology," http://www.itsma.com/pdfs/research/ITSMA_MarketingTechUserSurvey_AbbSum.pdf.
10. Active International (2014, March), "CMOs & CFOs Collision or Collaboration," http://www.activeinternational.com/~/media/Documents/ActiveInternationalSurveyReport0514.ashx.
11. Ibid.
12. Association of National Advertisers (ANA) (2014, July 24), "The New Role of Marketing: Survey Report Infographic," http://www.ana.net/miccontent/show/id/mkting2020-new-role-of-marketing-infographics.

6 Aligning Content to Your Buyer

1. CEB (2012), *The Digital Evolution in B2B Marketing.* Arlington, VA.
2. Content Marketing Institute, "What Is Content Marketing?" www.contentmarketinginstitute.com/what-is-content-marketing/.
3. ANNUITAS (2014), *Enterprise B2B Demand Generation Study.* Atlanta, GA.
4. DemandGen Report (2013), *2013 B2B Content Preferences Survey.* Hasbrouk Heights, NJ.
5. CEB (2012), ibid.
6. ANNUITAS (2014), ibid.
7. Ibid.
8. Spenner. P. (2014, July 23), "Demand Generation: How to Do It Right," CEB blog, https://www.executiveboard.com/blogs/demand-generation-how-to-do-it-right/.
9. News.com.au (2014, May 04), "E-mails Expected to Rise to 140 a Day in 2018," http://www.news.com.au/finance/work/emails-expected-to-rise-to-140-a-day-in-2018/story-e6frfm9r-1226904239876.
10. DemandGen Report (2013), ibid.
11. Lillian, J. (2013, May 9), "Summit 2013 Highlights: Inciting a B-to-B Content Revolution," *Sirius Decisions Blog*, https://www.siriusdecisions.com/Blog/2013/May/Summit-2013-Highlights-Inciting-a-BtoB-Content-Revolution.aspx.

7 Adapting the Lead Management Process

1. Bulldog Solutions, Frost & Sullivan. (2010). *The Executive Benchmark Assessment.* Austin, TX: Bulldog Solutions and Frost & Sullivan.
2. Gartner (2009), "Gartner Identifies the Top Six CRM Marketing Processes for a Cost-Constrained Economy," http://www.gartner.com/newsroom/id/862612.
3. Regalix Research (2014, March), *State of Marketing Automation 2014.* Palo Alto, CA.
4. ANNUITAS (2014), *Enterprise B2B Demand Generation Study.* Atlanta, GA.
5. DemandGen Report (2015, February). *2015 Content Preferences Survey.* Hasbrouk Heights, NJ.

6. ANNUITAS (2014), *Enterprise B2B Demand Generation Study*. Atlanta, GA.
7. Ibid.
8. Formstack (2015), *The 2015 Form Conversion Report*. Indianapolis, IN.
9. Rothman, D. (2013, February 27), "Landing Page Techniques That Drive Higher Conversion," *Marketo Blog*, http://blog.marketo.com/2013/02/landing -page-techniques-that-drive-higher-conversion.html.
10. American Marketing Association (AMA) (2013, January), "The Sales Lead Black Hole: On Sales' Reps Follow-Up of Marketing Leads," http://journals .ama.org/doi/abs/10.1509/jm.10.0047.
11. ANNUITAS (2014), ibid.
12. Marketing Sherpa (2012), "2012 B2B Marketing Benchmark Report," http://ftp.marketingsherpa.com/Marketing%20Files/PDF's/Executive%20 Summary/2012B2BBRMExcerpt.pdf.

8   Measuring for Success

1. ITSMA and Vision Edge Marketing (2014, June 10), "The Link between Marketing Performance Management and Value Creation," abbreviated summary. Lexington, MA.
2. Duke Fuqua School of Business, American Marketing Association, and McKinsey & Company (2015, February), *CMO Survey Report: Highlights and Insights*.
3. Fournaise Marketing Group (2104, April 8), "90% of Marketers Are Not Trained in Marketing Performance and Marketing ROI," https://www.four naisegroup.com/marketers-not-trained-in-marketing-performance-and-roi/.
4. ANNUITAS (2014), *Enterprise B2B Demand Generation Study*. Atlanta, GA.
5. Content Marketing Institute (2015), *B2B Content Marketing Benchmarks, Budgets & Trends*, http://contentmarketinginstitute.com/wp-content/uploads/2014/10 /2015_B2B_Research.pdf.
6. ANNUITAS (2014), ibid.
7. Ibid.
8. Ibid.
9. Vanboskirk, S. (2006, April 27), "The Reality of Marketing Metrics," http:// blogs.forrester.com/shar_vanboskirk/06-04-27-reality_marketing_metrics.

9   Optimizing Data and Technology

1. NetProspex (2014), *Annual Marketing Data Benchmark Report*.
2. Experian Data Quality (2014, January), *Making Your Data Work for You*.
3. Koetsier, J. (2014, January 20) "50% of Companies Use Multiple Marketing Automation Systems: VB Marketing Automation Index Update," *VentureBeat Blog*, http://venturebeat.com/2014/01/20/50-of-companies-use-multiple-marketing -automation-systems-vb-marketing-automation-index-update/.
4. Graber, R. (2012, March 08), "Your Marketing Database is Growing: Now What?" *Sirius Decisions Blog*, https://www.siriusdecisions.com/Blog/2012/Mar /Your-Marketing-Database-Is-Growing--Now-What.aspx.

5. ANNUITAS (2014), *Enterprise B2B Demand Generation Study*. Atlanta, GA.
6. Ibid.
7. DemandGen Report (2015), *Benchmark Study: What's Working in Demand Generation*. Hasbrouk Heights, NJ.
8. Experian Data Quality (2015, January), *The Data Quality Benchmark Report*. Boston, MA.

10   Creating an Outcome: Accountable Culture

1. The Fournaise Marketing Group (2014, January 23), "Over 70% of Marketers (Still) Got it Wrong in 2013." https://www.fournaisegroup.com/marketers-got -it-wrong-in-2013/.
2. ITSMA and Vision Edge Marketing (2014, June 10), "The Link between Marketing Performance Management and Value Creation," abbreviated summary. Lexington, MA.
3. Denning, S. (2011, July 23), "How Do You Change an Organizational Culture?" *Forbes*, http://www.forbes.com/sites/stevedenning/2011/07/23/how-do-you -change-an-organizational-culture/.
4. Ramos, Laura (2013), *B2B CMOs Must Evolve or Move On*. Cambridge, MA: Forrester.
5. Johnson, C. (2015, March 3), "Do Marketers Suffer From Performance Anxiety?" LinkedIn, https://www.linkedin.com/pulse/do-marketers-suffer-from -performance-anxiety-carla-johnson.
6. The Fournaise Marketing Group (2014, April 08). "90% of Marketers are Not Trained in Marketing Performance & Marketing ROI," https://www.fournaise group.com/marketers-not-trained-in-marketing-performance-and-roi/.
7. Forrester (2013), ibid.
8. B2B Marketing (2014, February 11), *Professional Development Benchmarking Report* (Infographic), http://www.b2bmarketing.net/content/pdfs/infographic -b2b%20marketing-skills-large.pdf.
9. ANNUITAS (2014), *Enterprise B2B Demand Generation Study*. Atlanta, GA.

11   Managing People through Change

1. Heath, C., and D. Heath (2010), *Switch: How to Change Things When Change is Hard*. New York: Broadway Books.
2. Appleinsider (2013, February 12), "Tim Cook: Apple's culture of innovation refuses to recognize any limits," http://appleinsider.com/articles/13/02/12/cook -apples-culture-of-innovation-refuses-to-recognize-limits, retrieved August 21, 2013.
3. Anderson, N. (1971), "Integration Theory and Attitude Change," *Psychological Review* 78 (3): 171–206.
4. Communication Institute for Online Scholarship. "Information Integration Theory," http://www.cios.org/encyclopedia/persuasion/Finformation_integration _2suggestions.htm.
5. Heath and Heath, *Switch*.

6. Ibid., 162.

7. Lombardo and Eichinger (2000), "High Potential as High Learners: Human Resource Management." *Human Resource Management* 39 (4): 321–30.

8. Mitchinson, A., and R. Morris (2012, April), *Learning About Learning Agility.* Greensboro, NC: Center for Creative Leadership.

9. Ibid.

10. Ibid.

11. De Meuse, K., D. Guangrong, and G. Hallenbeck (2010), "Learning Agility: A Construct Whose Time Has Come." *Consulting Psychology Journal: Practice and Research* 62 (2): 119–30.

12   The Need for Change

1. DemandGen Report (2015, February), *Content Preferences Survey.* Hasbrouk Heights, NJ.

2. Ibid.

3. Huff, D., and KOMarketing Associates (2014, February), "2014 B2B Web Usability Report: What B2B Buyers Want From Vendor Websites," www .komarketingassociates.com/b2b-web-usability-report-2014.

4. Rose, R. (2014, September 22), Chief Strategy Officer, Content Marketing Institute. C. Hidalgo, interviewer, Colorado Springs, CO.

13   Change Ahead

1. Ramos, Laura (2013), "B2B CMOs Must Evolve or Move On" Cambridge, MA: Forrester.

2. Ellet, J. (2015, January 1), "IDC Predicts Turmoil for CMOs in 2015," *Forbes,* http://www.forbes.com/sites/johnellett/2015/01/01/idc-predicts-turmoil-for -cmos-in-2015/.

3. Industry analyst (2013, November 19), C. Hidalgo, interviewer, San Francisco, CA.

4. Ibid.

5. Adkins-Green, S. (2015, March 29), "Applying the Change Agenda at Mary Kay," (D. Nessier, interviewer), *The Drew Blog,* http://www.thedrewblog.com /index.php/2015/03/29/applying-the-change-agenda-at-mary-kay/.

Bibliography

20, B2B Marketing's. *Infographic*. PDF. London: B2B Marketing, February 11, 2014.

2013 B2B Content Preferences Survey. Report. 2013. http://www.demandgenreport.com/industry-resources/research/2154-demand-gen-reports-2013-content-preferences-survey-examines-latest-content-trends.html.

"2015 Content Preferences Survey: Buyers Value Content Packages, Interactive Content." Demand Gen Report. March 4, 2015. http://www.demandgenreport.com/industry-resources/research/3141-2015-content-preferences-survey-buyers-value-content-packages-interactive-content-.html.

"2015 Form Conversion Report." Formstack. Accessed March 03, 2015. https://www.formstack.com/report/form-conversion-2015.

Adkins-Green, Sheryl. "Applying the Change at Mary Kay." Interview by Drew Nessier. The Drew Blog. March 29, 2015. http://www.thedrewblog.com/index.php/2015/03/29/applying-the-change-agenda-at-mary-kay/.

Anderson, Norman. "Integration Theory and Attitude Change." *Psychological Review* 78, no. 3 (1971): 171–206.

B2B Content Marketing Benchmarks, Budgets & Trends. Report. Accessed September 30, 2014. http://contentmarketinginstitute.com/wp-content/uploads/2014/10/2015_B2B_Research.pdf.

Brinker, Scott. "Marketing Technology Landscape Supergraphic." Chart. Chiefmartec.com. January 2015. http://cdn.chiefmartec.com/wp-content/uploads/2015/01/marketing_technology_jan2015.png.

Cespedes, Frank. *2012 B2B Marketing Benchmark Report*. Report. Accessed August 08, 2012. http://ftp.marketingsherpa.com/Marketing%20Files/PDF's/Executive%20Summary/2012B2BBRMExcerpt.pdf.

"CMOs & CFOs Collision or Collaboration." Active International. March 2014. http%3A%2F%2Fwww.activeinternational.com%2F~%2Fmedia%2FDocuments%2FActiveInternationalSurveyReport0514.ashx.

Cooperstein, David. "Marketing Change Management: Like It or Not, You Have to Figure It Out." Forbes. July 11, 2012. http://www.forbes.com/sites/davidcooperstein/2012/07/11/marketing-change-management-like-it-or-not-you-have-to-figure-it-out/.

The Data Quality Benchmark Report. Report. January 2015. https://www.edq.com /globalassets/whitepapers/data-quality-benchmark-report.pdf.

De Meuse, Kenneth P., Dai Guangrong, and George S. Hallenbeck. "Learning Agility: A Construct Whose Time Has Come." *Consulting Psychology Journal* 62, no. 2 (2010): 119–30.

Denning, Steve. "How Do You Change an Organizational Culture?" Forbes. July 7, 2011. http://www.forbes.com/sites/stevedenning/2011/07/23/how-do-you-change -an-organizational-culture/.

Dilger, Daniel Eran. "Tim Cook: Apple's Culture of Innovation Refuses to Recognize Any Limits." February 12, 2013. http://appleinsider.com/articles/13/02/12/cook -apples-culture-of-innovation-refuses-to-recognize-limits.

Ellet, John. "IDC Predicts Turmoil for CMOs in 2015." Forbes. January 1, 2015. http://www.forbes.com/sites/johnellett/2015/01/01/idc-predicts-turmoil-for -cmos-in-2015/.

"Emails Expected to Rise to 140 a Day in 2018." NewsComAu. May 4, 2014. http:// www.news.com.au/finance/work/emails-expected-to-rise-to-140-a-day-in-2018/ story-e6frfm9r-1226904239876.

Enterprise B2B Demand Generation Study. Report. October 28, 2014. http:// go.annuitas.com/l/16732/2014-11-05/dd3lr.

The Executive Benchmark Assessment. Report. Accessed December 5, 2010.

"FournaiseTrack: Media Releases." 80% of CEOs Do Not Really Trust Marketers (Except If They Are "ROI Marketers®"). July 10, 2012. https://www.fournaiseg roup.com/ceos-do-not-trust-marketers/.

"FournaiseTrack: Media Releases." 90% of Marketers Are Not Trained in Marketing Performance and Marketing ROI. April 08, 2014. https://www.fournaisegroup .com/marketers-not-trained-in-marketing-performance-and-roi/.

"FournaiseTrack: Media Releases." Over 70% of Marketers (Still) Got It Wrong in 2013. January 23, 2014. https://www.fournaisegroup.com/marketers-got-it -wrong-in-2013/.

"Gartner Identifies the Top Six CRM Marketing Processes for a Cost-Constrained Economy." January 22, 2009. http://www.gartner.com/newsroom/id/862612.

Graber, Ross. "SiriusDecisions." *Your Marketing Database Is Growing.* March 8, 2012. https://www.siriusdecisions.com/Blog/2012/Mar/Your-Marketing-Database -Is-Growing--Now-What.aspx.

Heath, Chip and Dan Heath. *Switch: How to Change Things When Change Is Hard.* New York: Broadway Books, 2010.

Huff, Dianna. *2014 B2B Web Usability Report.* Report. Boston: KOMarketing Associates, 2014.

"Information Integration Theory." Accessed February 12, 2014. http://www.cios .org/encyclopedia/persuasion/Finformation_integration_1theory.htm.

"Interview with Industry Analyst." Telephone interview by author. November 19, 2013.

Johnson, Carla. "Do Marketers Suffer from Performance Anxiety?" LinkedIn. March 3, 2015. https://www.linkedin.com/pulse/do-marketers-suffer-from-performance -anxiety-carla-johnson.

Koetsier, John. "50% of Companies Use Multiple Marketing Automation Systems: VB Marketing Automation Index Update." VentureBeat. January 20, 2014. http://venturebeat.com/2014/01/20/50-of-companies-use-multiple-marketing -automation-systems-vb-marketing-automation-index-update/.

Lillian, Jessica. "SiriusDecisions." *Summit 2013 Highlights: Inciting a B-to-B Content Revolution.* May 9, 2013. https://www.siriusdecisions.com/Blog/2013/May /Summit-2013-Highlights-Inciting-a-BtoB-Content-Revolution.aspx.

Lombardo, Michael and Robert Eichinger. "High Potentials as High Learners." *Human Resource Management* 39, no. 4 (January 8, 2001): 321–29. doi:10.1111/ (issn)1748–8583.

Making Your Data Work for You. Report. Accessed February 2014. http://cdn. qas.com/media/marketing/downloads/pdf/whitepapers/uk/v6_WP_Landscape -12pp-Ext-Jan13.pdf.

Maycock, Molly, Patrick Spenner, Robert Hamshar, Shelley West, and Nidhi Vikram Chodhury. *The Digital Evolution in B2b Marketing.* Report. Accessed December 5, 2014. http://www.executiveboard.com/exbd-resources/content/digi tal-evolution/pdf/Digital-Evolution-in-B2B-Marketing.pdf.

McLellan, Laura. "By 2017 the CMO Will Spend More on IT than the CIO ..." Gartner Webinars. January 3, 2012. http://my.gartner.com/portal/server.pt%3F open%3D512%26objID%3D202%26mode%3D2%26PageID%3D5553%26ref %3Dwebinar-rss%26resId%3D1871515.

Mitchinson, Adam and Robert Morris. *Learning about Learning Agility.* Report. April 2012.

Moorman, Christine. *The CMO Survey.* Report. February 2015. http://cmosurvey .org/results/.

Needles, Adam. "Is the CMO the Problem?" Editorial. Demand Gen Report, August 28, 2013. http://www.demandgenreport.com/industry-topics/demand ing-views/2296-is-the-cmo-the-problem.html.

"The New Role of Marketing Survey Report." Association of National Advertisers. July 16, 2014. http://www.ana.net/miccontent/show/id/mkting2020-the-new -role-of-marketing-survey.

Panayi, Nick. "Interview with Nick Panayi." Telephone interview by author. November 5, 2014.

Perkin, Neil and Heather Hopkins. *Skills of the Modern Marketer Report.* Report. May 2014. https://econsultancy.com/reports/skills-of-the-modern-marketer/.

Raab, David. *Raab Vest Report.* Report. Accessed December 5, 2014. http://raab guide.com/vest.

Ramos, Laura. *B2B CMOs Must Evolve or Move On.* Report. July 3, 2013. https:// solutions.forrester.com/bma-survey-findings-ramos.

Rose, Robert. "Interview with Robert Rose." Telephone interview by author. September 22, 2014.

Rothman, Dayna. "Landing Page Techniques That Drive Higher Conversion." *Marketo Marketing Blog Best Practices and Thought Leadership.* February 27, 2013. http://blog.marketo.com/2013/02/landing-page-techniques-that-drive-higher -conversion.html.

Sabnis, Gaurav, Sharmila C. Chatterjee, Rajdeep Grewal, and Gary L. Lilien. "The Sales Lead Black Hole: On Sales Reps' Follow-Up of Marketing Leads." *AMA Journals*. January 2013. http://journals.ama.org/doi/abs/10.1509/jm.10.0047.

Schwartz, Julie and Dan Armstrong. *Realizing the Promise of Marketing Technology*. Report. March 2013. http://www.itsma.com/pdfs/research/ITSMA _MarketingTechUserSurvey_AbbSum.pdf.

Schwartz, Julie and Laura Patterson. "Marketing Performance Management and Value Creation." ITSMA. June 4, 2014. http://www.itsma.com/research/2014 -itsma-vem-marketing-performance-management-survey/.

Spenner, Patrick. "Demand Generation: How to Do It Right." CEB Blogs. July 23, 2104. https://www.executiveboard.com/blogs/demand-generation-how-to-do-it -right/.

"State of Marketing Automation 2014." Regalix Research. 2014. http://www.rega lix.com/by_regalix/research/reports/state-of-marketing-automation-2014/.

"The State of Marketing Data." NetProspex. Accessed Winter 2014. http://pages .netprospexinc.com/Marketing-Data-Benchmark-Report.html.

Unlock Your Potential in 2015: CEB Sales, Service, Marketing, Communication. Report. 2015. Accessed January 26, 2015. https://www.cebglobal.com/exbd/sales -service/year-in-preview/index.page?cid=701800000019jkRAAQ.

Van Meurs, Bert. "CMO Lessons in Working with a CEO." Interview by Tom French. McKinsey. April 2014. http://www.mckinseyonmarketingandsales.com /cmo-lessons-in-working-with-a-ceo.

Vanboskirk, Sahr. "Shar VanBoskirk's Blog." *The Reality of Marketing Metrics*. April 27, 2006. http://blogs.forrester.com/shar_vanboskirk/06-04-27-reality _marketing_metrics.

Vohra, Nimish and Srinivasan Seethapathy. *State of B2B Marketing 2015*. Report. December 2014. http://www.regalix.com/by_regalix/research/reports/state-of -b2b-marketing-2015/.

"What Is Content Marketing?" Content Marketing Institute. April 16, 2014. http:// www.contentmarketinginstitute.com/what-is-content-marketing/.

"What Is Social Selling? Connections and Content." Forbes. May 8, 2013. http:// www.forbes.com/sites/sap/2013/05/08/what-is-social-selling-connections-and -content/.

What's Working in B2B Demand Generation. Report. January 28, 2015. http://www .demandgenreport.com/industry-resources/research/3090-2015-benchmark -study-whats-working-in-demand-generation.html.

Whipple, Brian and Baiju Shah. *The CMO-CIO Disconnect: Bridging the Gap to Seize the Digital Opportunity*. Report. Accessed September 03, 2013. https:// www.google.com/url?sa=t&rct=j&q=&esrc=s&source=web&cd=7&cad=rja&u act=8&ved=0CEQQFjAGahUKEwiPpNL5nPTGAhUDrIAKHcKaAQ0&ur l=http%3A%2F%2Fwww.accenture.com%2Fnl-en%2FPages%2Finsight-cmo -cio-bridging-gap-seize-digital-opportunity.aspx&ei=92yyVc_MIoPYggTCtYZ o&usg=AFQjCNFacTBm4ZQLv0BO6kh7ZC2IodhgAA&sig2=Sp-8XDg8k -_8MnGKFQSn7Q&bvm=bv.98476267,d.eXY.

Index